HI
BEXAR COUNTY
An Illustrated History

by Joe Carroll Rust

Published for the Bexar County Historical Commission

Historical Publishing Network
A division of Lammert Incorporated
San Antonio, Texas

Second Edition

Copyright © 2006 Historical Publishing Network

All rights reserved. No part of this book may be reproduced in any form or by any means, electronic or mechanical, including photocopying, without permission in writing from the publisher. All inquiries should be addressed to Historical Publishing Network, 11555 Galm Road, Suite 100, San Antonio, Texas, 78254. Phone (800) 749-0464.

ISBN: 9781893619579
Library of Congress Card Catalog Number: 2006925917

Historic Bexar County: An Illustrated History

author:	Joe Carroll Rust
cover artist:	Vanessa Lively

Historical Publishing Network

president:	Ron Lammert
project managers:	Curtis Courtney
	Sydney McNew
	Roger Smith
	Pat Steele
administration:	Donna M. Mata
book sales:	Dee Steidle
production:	Colin Hart
	Charles Newton III

Contents

4	Preface	*a word beforehand*
6	Chapter I	*in the beginning*
16	Chapter II	*independence and its aftermath*
24	Chapter III	*courthouses, travellers, trails, tracks*
44	Chapter IV	*generals, teachers, and preachers*
72	Chapter V	*the golden age in Bexar*
88	Chapter VI	*into surburbia*
108	Chapter VII	*the river: the stream of life*
118	Chapter VIII	*Bexar County comes of age*
144	Resources	
146	Appendices	
150	About the Author	
151	About the Cover	

PREFACE

A Word Beforehand

This is the story of the millions of people who traveled through a river valley in South Central Texas over a period of up to ten thousand years. Some trekked on through, but some stayed and created a unique society.

This is the story of Bexar County, one of the 254 counties in the state of Texas. It is the home of San Antonio, ninth largest city in population in the United States, and also of 24 incorporated suburban cities all or in part within its limits. It is also home to four major military installations and at least a dozen other well-established unincorporated communities. Of the 1,248 square miles comprising Bexar County, more than 575 square miles remain beyond the incorporated cities and the military bases.

There has long been a controversy over the spelling of Bexar. David P. Green, in *Place Names of San Antonio*, explains it this way, "The letter 'x' in old Spanish was the phonetic equivalent of 'j' in so-called modern Spanish. Thus 'Bexar' is the old Spanish spelling of modern Spanish 'Bejar.' The correct pronunciation for both is BAY-har. Why and when did the 'x' become silent? The most likely answer is that Anglo settlers in Texas had trouble pronouncing the harsh Spanish 'j.' Linguists refer to such speech patterns as 'phonetic drift,' but it is not clear when the transition to the current pronunciation of 'Bear' took place." The name "Bejar" (Bexar) was to honor the Duque de Bejar, brother of the Spanish viceroy, who died defending Budapest from the Turks in 1686.

Bexar County lies at the edge of the Balcones Escarpment, the land ranging from the foothills of the Hill Country in the north to the flatness of the Coastal Plain in the south. Part of the county is over the Edwards Plateau, with its numerous springs, artesian and underground wells and aquifers that provide the area's major source of drinking water.

The county's population in the 2000 census was 1,392,931, with 1,144,646 living in San Antonio (another 50,000 had been added by July 2002). According to the U.S. Census, the county's racial and ethnic makeup is 54.35 percent Hispanic, 36.33 non-Hispanic Anglo, 7.20 African American, and 2.12 other, including Orientals and Native Americans.

This narrative shows that history, even though often keyed to specific events and ideas, really is a continuum. For Bexar County, it is a flow that daily leaves an enriching cultural silt, much like the river which has been so valuable to the county's community. History is not static, but ever movable, ever on-going.

This is a history of recurring themes, of Bexar County moving forward in "clumps" of development around certain geographic locations, including waterways, and around certain prominent families. Such terms as "adaptive reuse" and "balance of preservation and progress" will become familiar to readers.

This is a survey history of how various groups moved into Central Texas and left their own cultures, a curious combination of mores and customs, joining the charm of the Old World, the roughness of the Southwest, and the gentility of the Old South.

This is a panoramic history. It is presented primarily in chronological form, but sometimes by necessity, topically. History does not always lend itself to date-by-date development. Some will call this work a "popular" history, a "generic" history, or a "coffee table" history, which suggests that it is fictional. It is not.

This story makes no pretense to be a definitive history of the county, addressing all events which have built it. Many wonderful books have been written, and continue to be written, about the rich history of San Antonio, especially of the historic structures and significant battles which formed the framework of the area's early days.

This is the first history written to address in brevity the totality of Bexar County's history. Yet, it barely scratches the surface. It is hoped that many of the points addressed in this work will whet the historic appetites of those who might take up its themes and develop them further. Nor is there an attempt here to address the many myths, overstatements and understatements of the county's history. The history of Bexar County is colorful enough without this.

Despite many centuries building the treasure trove of history, history continues to be a work in progress, in Bexar County and everywhere else. History is today.

To my darling wife Margie, who inspired me to write a better book, I dedicate this work.

So, the story begins.

Joe Carroll Rust
December 2004

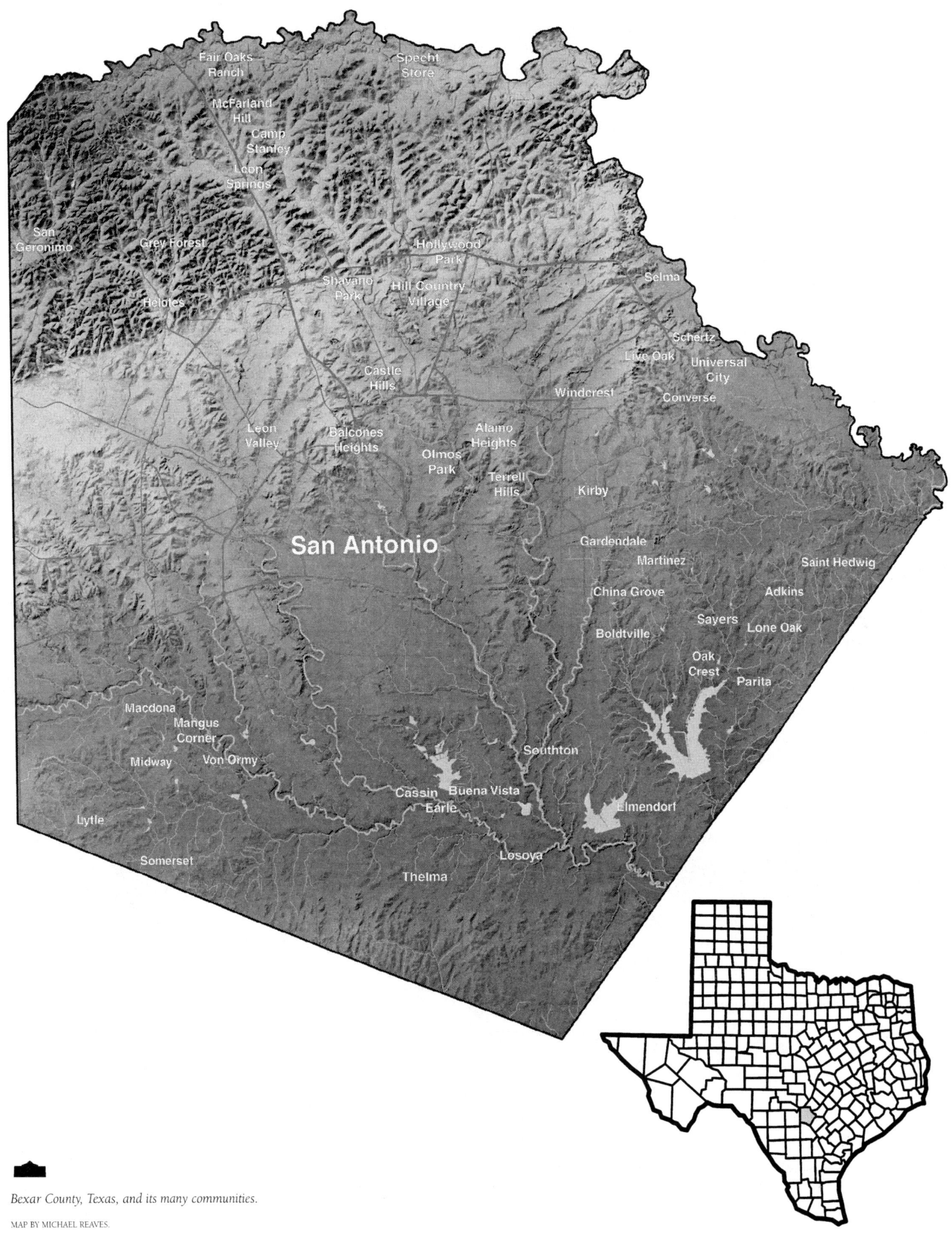

Bexar County, Texas, and its many communities.

MAP BY MICHAEL REAVES.

Chapter I

In the Beginning

It started, so it seems, up to ten thousand years ago during the Clovis culture in a fertile river valley in what now is north central Bexar County. Nomadic bands of Native American hunter/gatherers came to what is now called the Olmos Basin, where springs joined the headwaters of the river later to be called the San Antonio, to enjoy the rich vegetation and cool waters. The weather then, unaffected by any nearby development, probably was cooler, and enriching grasses taller and more plentiful.

Today, the basin is bounded on the north by "The Quarry Market," a commercial shopping mall carved out of a quarry, and rimmed by two suburban cities, Olmos Park and Alamo Heights, connected by the Olmos Dam. It gives way to the south to massive rock outcroppings, the source of building materials for many significant local buildings, including some of the Spanish missions. It separates two institutions of higher learning, the University of the Incarnate Word and Trinity University, and forms the northern boundary of the San Antonio Zoological Gardens, Brackenridge Park, and Brackenridge Golf Course. The landscape fades south into a level plain along U.S. Highway 281, a wide band of concrete and asphalt which cuts through the basin to connect the San Antonio International Airport and towns at the eastern edge of the Hill Country to the skyline of downtown San Antonio. Nearly five hundred caves are honeycombed throughout the county, the largest being Robber Baron Cave, just north of Alamo Heights.

On a drive along the highway through the basin, one easily can imagine how bands of Native Americans long ago could enjoy and gain sustenance from the green landscape. At the eastern edge of the basin, just a few blocks from Incarnate Word and the headwaters of the river, volunteer workers for the Episcopal Diocese of West Texas are building new nature trails into the basin, ripping out intrusive vegetation and restoring native grasses and plants to the area. The headquarters buildings of the diocese stand at the edge of this project.

There is no evidence that the bands of hunters/gatherers ever set up permanent camps in their wanderings through the basin. About three thousand years later, it appears their descendants did set up some permanent housekeeping in an area farther south along the river, near Leon Creek and the Medina River, in current southern Bexar County. These indigenous peoples, although enjoying a lifestyle considered primitive by twenty-first century standards, were comfortable with their locale. They spoke several distinct languages and they had their own separate gods, traditions and methods of survival.

These hunter/gatherers carried names found only in a few books—Pajalache, Aranama, Tamique, Pachal, Suliajam, Jaunae, Pantaya, Arbadao, Katuhano, Cacaxtle, Pampoa, Cotzal, Queven. Their names vanished one by one, melding later into the Coahuiltecan and Tonkawan peoples. Some were overtaken later by the Lipan Apaches and Comanches who were more warlike. The general reference to the Native Americans of this area evolved to "Coahuiltecans." The descendants of these early tribes laid the stones of the area's colonial missions for the European newcomers, the Spanish, in the 17th and 18th centuries. Visitors to communities around the missions today can imagine in the large and bright eyes of youngsters a glimpse of the gentle souls and quiet lifestyle of those who lived in the region before the outside world brought poverty and pestilence. Before this time, most wars they knew were for survival, not for conquest.

It was into the simple lives of these early dwellers that the Spanish explorers brought a new religion, new weapons and the horse-mounted Spaniards to impose a new kind of lifestyle on them. The hunter/gatherers succumbed to the invaders because they wanted to save their declining civilization. Unfortunately, the new wave of invasion, under the banner of a foreign king, almost destroyed them. Their story of demise is told with poignancy in *Gente de razón*, a film

Opposite: Olmos Dam now spans the Olmos Basin, where Native Americans trekked ten thousand years ago.

Above: Camp of the Lipans, by Theodore Gentilz, shows the lifestyle of early Native Americans in Bexar County.
COURTESY OF THE WITTE MUSEUM, SAN ANTONIO, TEXAS.

Below: Lookout Mountain in northern Bexar County was a scouting area for the Comanches.

shown at The Visitors Center for San Antonio Missions National Historical Park located at Mission San José.

The first European explorers to encounter the hunter/gatherers of the San Antonio River Valley may have been Alvar Nuñez Cabeza de Vaca and his two companions, who were shipwrecked and taken captive by Native Americans. In the 1520s he visited the interior of Texas and mapped rivers, one of which may have been the San Antonio. Mary Ann Noonan Guerra noted in The San Antonio River that if he did camp at the headwaters of the river, San Antonio should be listed as "one of the oldest historical sites in North America." Guerra also pointed out that some historians believe that Alonso de León, who became the governor of Coahuila and Texas, may have camped at the headwaters of the river as early as 1670. "But it wasn't until 1691 that the documented chronicle of this river began," she wrote.

Incursions of the French spurred the Spanish movements from Mexico into present-day Texas in the late seventeenth century. In 1695, Rene Robert Cavalier, Sieur de La Salle, having not satisfied the French monarch after finding the mouth of the Mississippi River, returned to the New World. La Salle had participated in an expedition that descended the Mississippi to its mouth. He was sent with the express purpose of planting a "colony" on the coast to make inroads into territory claimed by Spain and to lay the foundation for cutting off the northern silver mining of New Spain. In his new voyage, he overshot the mouth of the Mississippi by six hundred miles to the west, landing at Matagorda Bay on the Texas coast. Even though he encountered alligators, swarms of mosquitoes and a Texas norther that sank one of his ships, he built Fort St. Louis on East Texas soil. The Spanish reacted in a decision to investigate the land they had claimed many years before, but had not explored, and so began sending expeditions north. As it was, much of the Spanish settlement of Texas for well beyond one hundred years was a result of pressure from the French in western Louisiana.

In "The Mission Era: The Finding of Texas, 1519-1693" Volume 1 of *Our Catholic Heritage in Texas, 1519-1936*, Carlos E. Castañeda explains in detail how De León, in the late 1680s and the early 1690s, led five expeditions into Texas in search of the French Fort St. Louis. He found the fort on his fourth expedition and destroyed it on his fifth expedition. His recommendation that Spain take steps for the formal occupation of Texas, in the face of the French incursions, led to the establishment of Spanish missions in East Texas. His later recommendation that settlements and a line of Spanish presidios, or forts, be established gave way to a recommendation by Fray Damián Massanet. This Franciscan missionary who had accompanied De León recommended that the Spanish presence in Texas be limited to the missions, dedicated to the conversion of the Native Americans to Christianity.

The first outsiders to definitely see the Bexar indigenous population were Domingo Terán de los Ríos, who succeeded De León as "the governor of Tejas and adjacent regions," according to Castañeda, and Fray Massanet. On June 13, 1691, they reached a waterway near where Mission San Juan Capistrano later was founded. The local Payaya Indians called the river Yanaguana. In his *San Antonio, a Unique History and Pictorial Guide*, Henry Guerra refers to Yanaguana as "a place of pleasant waters." Fray Massanet, recognizing June 13 as the feast day of Saint Anthony, celebrated Mass and renamed the place San Antonio de Padua. From this, one might have projected the international nature of what was to become San Antonio. To this day, the city boasts one of the most cosmopolitan populations of any major city in North America.

Spanish expeditions through San Antonio in 1709 and 1714 to assess where best to plant missions, and along with them, the requisite presidio, brought about the naming of San Pedro Springs. It was clear from the beginning that the building of both the presidios and the missions was not necessarily a matter of defense, but a way to expand the borders of New Spain and secure a hold on a new dominion, keeping it out of the hands of the French. Mother Church was dedicated to converting the Native Americans to Roman Catholicism.

During the first week of May, 1718, considered by many historians the official beginning of San Antonio, Martín de Alarcón, the first Spanish governor of Texas when its administration was separated from that of Coahuila, established the mission and presidio south of San Pedro Springs. He named it San Antonio de Bejar. The Spanish moved the

Rene Robert Cavalier, Sieur de La Salle, landed in Texas in the late 1600s. This engraving is based on a 1865 painting by Leon Mayer that was based on a portrait in Pierre Margry's Memoires et Documents Pour Servir a l'Histoire des Irigines Francaises des Pays d'Outremer, Fortier, Alcee. A History of Louisiana.

COURTESY OF THE INSTITUTE OF TEXAN CULTURES AT THE UNIVERSITY OF TEXAS AT SAN ANTONIO.

Above: Mission San Jose, known as the "queen of missions," c. 1945.
COURTESY OF THE INSTITUTE OF TEXAN CULTURES AT THE UNIVERSITY OF TEXAS AT SAN ANTONIO.

Below: The Alamo as it appears today.

Mission of San Francisco de Solano from the Rio Grande Valley to near the presidio site. The new complex took on the name San Antonio de Valero, in honor of San Antonio and the viceroy Marquis de Valero. In 1722, the presidio was moved to *Plaza de Armas*, Military Plaza, near the present-day San Antonio City Hall and later the site of the Spanish Governor's Palace. Above the doorway of that palace still exists the only stone replica of the Hapsburg crest in the Northern Hemisphere. Some of the families of the presidio soldiers lived in La Villita, a small settlement on the river which resisted frequent flooding because it was on higher ground. The small civilian support community that grew up near the presidio of San Antonio de Bejar later was absorbed by the Canary Island settlement of the Villa de San Fernando. In 1719, Mission San Antonio de Valero was moved to a site on the east bank of the river near the present-day St. Joseph's Catholic Church. When that building was destroyed in a severe storm in 1724, the mission was moved to its present-day location on Alamo Plaza.

In 1720 the second of the Bexar missions, San José y San Miguel de Aguayo, was founded by Father Margil de Jesús. Mission San Francisco de Nájera was formed as a sub-mission of Valero, established to accommodate a group of natives that did not want to reside with the other group. After a short time, the disagreement was forgiven, and some of those at Nájera went to Valero. The rest returned to the wilderness. A temporary truce between Spain and France caused the closing of a presidio that had guarded the three missions, leaving them vulnerable to attack by the traditional enemies of the potential residents. The Spanish transferred three missions—Nuestra Señora de la Purísima Concepción de Acuña, San Francisco de la Espada, and San

Juan Capistrano—to Bexar County along the river. Espada (San Francisco de los Tejas) and Capistrano (San José de los Nazonis) bore different names while in East Texas. San José de los Nazonis was given the new name of Capistrano to avoid confusion with San José y San Miguel de Aguayo.

Thus, Bexar County with five missions has a more closely concentrated number of Spanish colonial missions than any other area in North America. The church at Concepción is the oldest unrestored and unchanged edifice of its kind in the United States. San José is known as the "Queen of the Missions." Through the years, after secularization by the church in the 1790s, the missions returned to church authority in the nineteenth century. In 1793, the Alamo was absorbed into the parish of San Fernando. In *The Alamo Chain of Missions*, Marion A. Habig wrote, "In 1794, the year after the suppression of Mission San Antonio de Valero, the other four (missions) were partially secularized; but they continued to be missions for another three decades until 1824, when the final secularization took place." In 1841, the Republic of Texas confirmed that the mission churches belonged to the Catholic Church, and in 1855 the Texas Supreme Court ruled in favor of church ownership after the City of San Antonio filed suit for the property. In 1877 the bishop of San Antonio, Anthony D. Pellicer, sold a portion of the mission property containing the convent building to Honore Grenet for $20,000, with the Catholic church retaining control of the

Above: Mission Espada, c. 1950s.
PHOTO BY HARVEY BELGIN. COURTESY OF THE INSTITUTE OF TEXAN CULTURES AT THE UNIVERSITY OF TEXAS AT SAN ANTONIO.

Below: Mission Espada today.
COURTESY OF THE ZINTGRAFF COLLECTION, INSTITUTE OF TEXAN CULTURES AT THE UNIVERSITY OF TEXAS AT SAN ANTONIO.

Above: Marriage Procession, Mission San Juan Capistrano (n.d.) by Louise Fretéllière. Her father had come to Texas with French Count Henri Castro in 1843. The Spanish brought Christianity to Texas in the sixteenth century, and their beautiful missions still dot the state.
COURTESY OF THE TORCH COLLECTION, HOUSTON, TEXAS.

Right: Mission Concepcion, c. 1920.
COURTESY OF THE UNIVERSITY OF THE INCARNATE WORD.

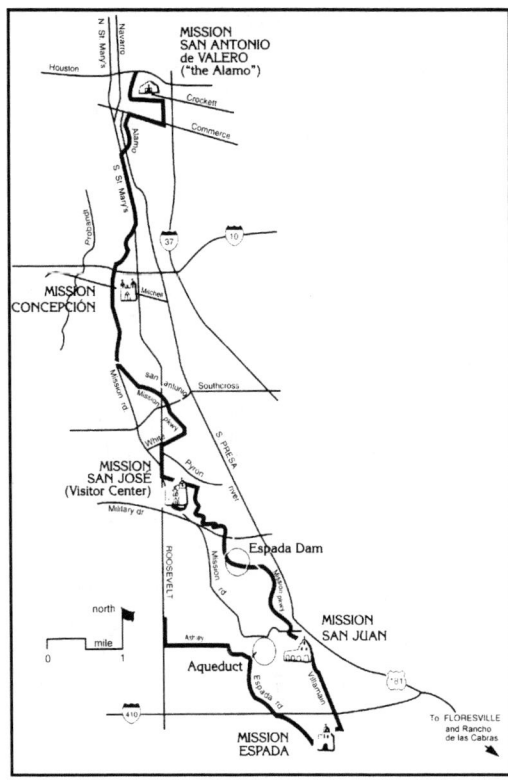

Left: A map showing the geographic relationship of the Bexar County Spanish missions to each other.
COURTESY OF THE SAN ANTONIO MISSIONS NATIONAL HISTORICAL PARK.

Above: San Fernando Church, c. 1868.
COURTESY OF THE SAN ANTONIO LIGHT COLLECTION, THE INSTITUTE OF TEXAN CULTURES AT THE UNIVERSITY OF TEXAS AT SAN ANTONIO.

Alamo church. In 1883, Bishop John C. Neraz sold the remainder of the Alamo property, containing the church, to the State of Texas, for another $20,000. In 1885 the state granted custodianship of the Alamo church to the City of San Antonio. For more than a half-century, ownership and/or control of various Alamo properties seesawed back and forth among private developers and governmental entities and finally to management by the Daughters of the Republic of Texas. Today, the missions are linked by a Mission Parkway and are part of a joint program in which the mission grounds are part of the National Park System, while the mission churches themselves are active Roman Catholic parishes. San Antonio de Valero—which became known as the Alamo—alone in downtown San Antonio remains apart from the other four and is not an active church.

While the missions were being put in place in Bexar, another significant development was taking place, another element to cement Spanish hold over the area. In 1723 the king of Spain, urged by the friars and the Council of the Indies among others, had issued a royal decree that a civil settlement be established near the Bejar presidio. He made plans for families to travel from the Spanish-held Canary Islands off the coast of Africa to Bexar. The Spanish had claimed these islands as early as 1407 and controlled them by 1491. The king made the offer attractive by pledging to fund their trip. He also gave them land and, probably more importantly for the farmers of the Canary Islands, a royal title. He dubbed each of them an *hidalgo*, a made-up term which loosely translated means "son of something," a term of lesser nobility, akin to "Sir" in England. Today, the Bexar County Commissioners Court issues the certificate of *hidalgo* to visiting personages, making them unofficial official members of royalty, and the San Antonio City Council dubs dignitaries as *alcaldes*, or mayors.

In 1724 the first Canary Island families began the trip, via Havana and Vera Cruz, then overland to San Antonio. There is some evidence that the destination of the Canary Islanders initially was not Bexar, but another mission area and that they wound up in San Antonio by mistake. On March 9, 1731, the first 15 Canary Islander families and one *bachelor* (56 people) arrived in San Antonio, naming their new home the Villa de San Fernando, in honor of King Fernando II of Spain. They established a city council, the *cabildo*, the first civil government in Texas. Several years later they began to lay out a Spanish colonial church on the west side of the Plaza de las Islas, just east of the presidio. The plots of land for the Canary Islanders had been designated before their arrival, stretching out from the site of the church. Why the newcomers did not build the

Chapter I ♦ 13

Above: San Fernando Cathedral and the Plaza de las Islas, c. the 1880s.
COURTESY OF JOHN AND DELA WHITE AND THE ZINTGRAFF COLLECTION, THE INSTITUTE OF TEXAN CULTURES AT THE UNIVERSITY OF TEXAS AT SAN ANTONIO.

Right: San Fernando Cathedral, 1978.
COURTESY OF JOHN AND DELA WHITE AND THE ZINTGRAFF COLLECTION, THE INSTITUTE OF TEXAN CULTURES AT THE UNIVERSITY OF TEXAS AT SAN ANTONIO.

Below: East Side of Main Plaza by W. G. M. Samuel, showing Casas Reales, the first Bexar County Courthouse.
COURTESY OF BEXAR COUNTY AND THE WITTE MUSEUM, SAN ANTONIO, TEXAS.

church on the east side of Plaza de las Islas, Main Plaza, matching the tradition in Spain to build the church on the east side of the plaza to recognize Christ as the rising sun, is unknown. Some villages in Mexico also did not follow the tradition.

The colonists designated the front steps of the colonial church, San Fernando, as the center of the city, declaring God the center of everything. More than a hundred years later, the colonial church became a cathedral, with a primarily French Gothic addition, becoming the longest continuously operated cathedral sanctuary in the United States and one of the oldest buildings in Texas.

As soon as the construction of the first missions had progressed sufficiently, the Jarame, Payaya, and Pamaya Indian groups had begun to move into the mission compounds. When the Canary Islanders, the *isleños*, arrived, the population included these Native Americans, soldiers, *bexarenos*, or citizens of Bexar, and cattlemen, or vaqueros. Relations at first were strained. Some in the existing Bexar population considered the *hidalgos* a bit "uppity," because they claimed some sort of nobility. Some of that resentment remains to this day, but eventually most of the cowboys and the farmers *did* become friends.

In 1742 the Canary Islanders erected their first government building, on the east side of the plaza, backed up to the river. Most government buildings in Spain are on the west side of the

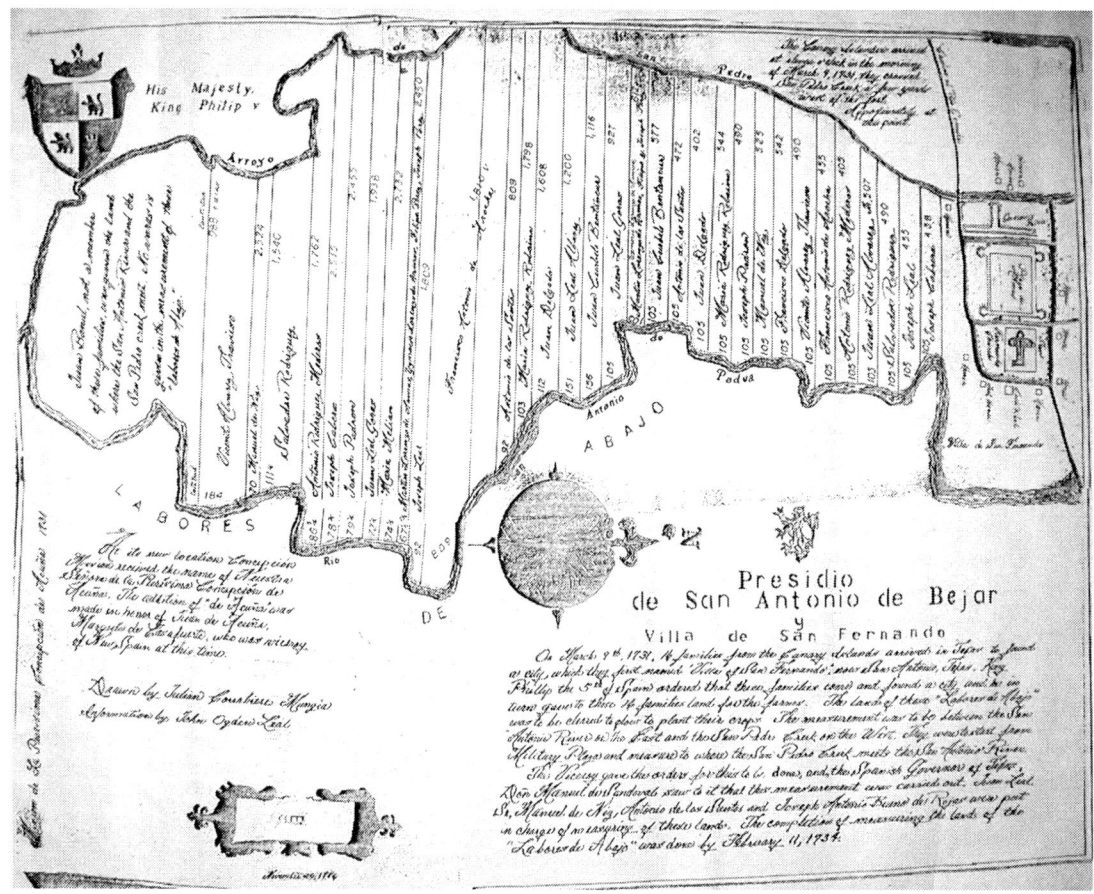

The plots of land for the Canary Islanders were laid out from the church.

COURTESY OF THE BEXAR COUNTY ARCHIVES

plaza. The building was *Casas Reales*, the first Bexar courthouse. It was on the corner of what is now Dolorosa and Dwyer, cater-cornered from what now is the county's courthouse. The construction of *Casas Reales* set in motion the "clump" or "cluster" nature of local governmental operations in Bexar County. All the courthouses built to serve the county or city halls built have been constructed within a two-block downtown area. For many years thereafter the villa, the missions and the presidio comprised the largest Spanish concentration in Texas, even becoming the provincial capital in 1772. Yet, Bexar remained a small frontier outpost.

Individual missions controlled large ranches, raising herds of cattle and other livestock. Only one of these ranches still exists, but only as a place on the map, a limited access archeology site, rather than a working ranch. It is *Rancho de las Cabras*, the Goat Ranch, which Espada used for grazing lands. During mission days, it was in Bexar County, but later realignments placed it in adjacent Wilson County. All of the missions operated as their own economic units but they held in common that water was necessary for survival. The Spanish constructed a system of *acequias*, or irrigation ditches, to provide water for all the missions and their farms and ranches. Each mission community and the Villa de San Fernando had its own irrigation system, with its own dam and system of *acequias*. In Espada's case, there also was an aqueduct transporting the water from the San Antonio River to that mission's farm fields over Piedras Creek.

When the missions were secularized, they became satellite communities to the villa. Disease and the raids of the Comanches and Apaches had decimated the populations, and the government divided the mission lands among the Native Americans who had built the missions and the increasing number of Spanish settlers. The Canary Islanders and soldiers controlled lands in the villa. Later, the mission irrigation system began to crumble and the total acreage of irrigated farmland began to dwindle, decreasing markedly by the time the new century dawned. Yet what was dawning was a new era which would catapult Bexar County into the history books forever. The nineteenth century was to be, as young people many years later were to say, "something else."

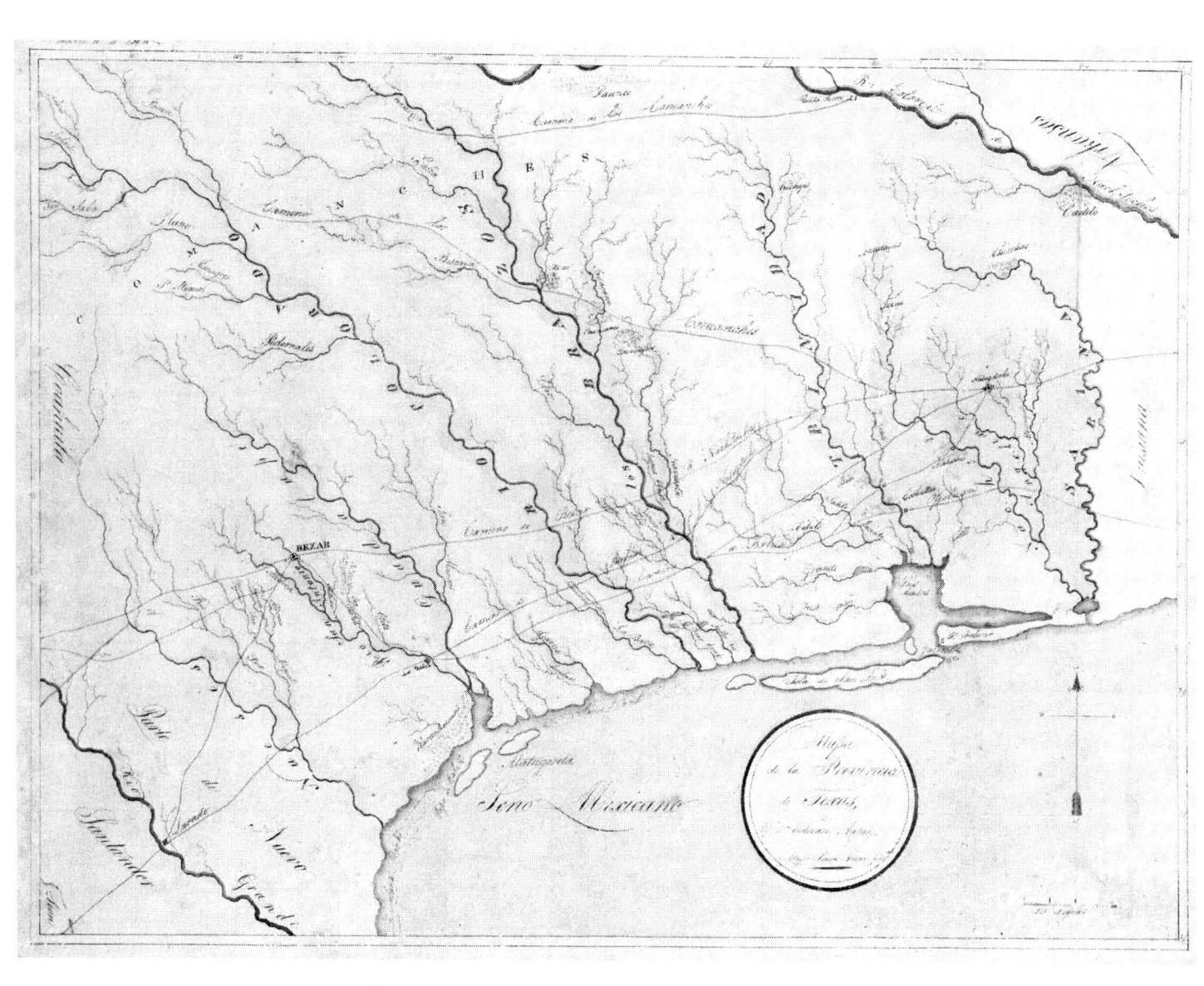

Chapter II

Independence and Its Aftermath

As Bexar County entered the 1800s, the community continued to be primarily agricultural. Yet it was becoming a main shipping point along *El Camino Real*, the King's Highway, which led from Mexico through San Antonio and Nacogdoches into Louisiana. South toward Mexico, there were grumblings of unrest, and the demand for change erupted in 1810, when on September 16, Father Miguel Hidalgo y Costilla, a Catholic priest, declared from the village of Dolores that Mexico should be, and would be, free of Spanish control. The movement for independence took 11 years, and Mexicans and those of Mexican heritage still celebrate September 16, *diez y seis*, in Mexico and the U.S. Southwest as Mexican Independence Day.

Of all the Spanish outposts in the north, Bexar County became one of the most prominent in revolutionary activity. The Hidalgo Revolt had a great impact on Texas and the San Antonio area. In 1811, poor soldiers and civilians who resented the rule of the Spanish elite, the Royalists, mounted an insurrection that failed because most of the *isleños*, conservative military officers and clergy refused to help. The Spanish executed the leader of the revolt, Juan Bautista de las Casas, in Mexico. They then salted and shipped his head in a box to Bexar to put on display on Military Plaza as a warning against further revolution. In truth, Las Casas and his followers were trying to settle scores with neighbors and confiscated their property as suspected insurrectionists. In a short time, there was dissension among Las Casas' followers and the "revolt" ended.

Festering resentment against Spanish rule erupted again in 1813, when Bernardo Gutiérrez de Lara and Augustus W. Magee led an expedition from Louisiana, capturing San Antonio. They executed Governor Manuel Salcedo and his military aide, Simón de Herrera, in retaliation for the arrest of Father Hidalgo and proclaimed Texas an independent state. The expedition hoisted the Green Flag. Some historians believe it should join the six flags which have flown over Texas—Spanish, French, Mexican, Republic of Texas, Confederate, and the U.S. In August 1813, however, all hope of the short-lived independence of Texas failed. Gutiérrez de Lara's men met the Spanish in a large field south of San Antonio, in what then was part of Bexar County (now Atascosa County) in the Battle of Medina, the largest battle ever fought on Texas soil. About 1,400 of the 2,000 men in Gutiérrez de Lara's forces lost their lives. One of the young officers of the much larger Spanish army at Medina was Antonio López de Santa Anna.

In the summer of 2003 some of the descendants of the Gutiérrez de Lara band met with major historians in Texas at the site of the battle and placed grave markers. An effort is being made to locate the descendants of those from both sides of this battle, one almost lost in the history books of Texas.

For almost a decade San Antonio languished in obscurity. In 1820, however, the population (then 1,021 females and 973 males in the villa, but rising on nearby ranches) took an upswing. That year, Moses Austin of Missouri arrived in San Antonio to petition the Spanish governor for a permit to settle Americans in Texas. Austin at first was rebuffed by the Spanish authorities, but finally was given the go-ahead for colonization. He was to bring three hundred moral, hardworking, Catholic families from the former Spanish territory of Louisiana to Texas under an *empresario* grant. Although the authorities wanted him to settle close to San Antonio, he opted for a still-to-be defined area along the lower Colorado River. He died in June 1821, leaving the plan to his eldest son, Stephen Fuller Austin.

Mexico secured its independence in 1821, thus also making Texas a land free of European control. Stephen F. Austin arrived in San Antonio in mid-1821 to petition the new Mexican governor to allow him to carry out his father's plans to bring in settlers. In April 1823 he finalized a contract under the Imperial Colonization Law. As the most successful Texas *empresario*, Austin made four six-year

A map of the Austin colonies in Texas.
COURTESY OF THE WITTE MUSEUM, SAN ANTONIO, TEXAS.

This painting by Theodore Gentilz gives a bird's-eye view of the Mexican army charging the Alamo. The painting was later destroyed by fire.
COURTESY OF THE INSTITUTE OF TEXAN CULTURES AT THE UNIVERSITY OF TEXAS AT SAN ANTONIO.

contracts between 1823 and 1825, for a potential 1,200 families. According to the *Handbook of Texas Online*, they were to settle "between the watersheds of the Brazos and Colorado Rivers and as far as the Lavaca River below the Old San Antonio Road, as well as eastward to the San Jacinto River (but not including Galveston Island) and a small area around the site of present-day Austin." In 1831 he was issued a fifth contract for eight hundred families to be settled along the Brazos above the Old Spanish Road. That contract faced a challenge from the holder of an expired prior claim. The Austin settlers arrived in 1825, a year after Texas and Coahuila had been combined into a geographically unified, but politically divergent, territory. The capital of the new Mexican state was established at Saltillo, because it was the administrative center for the Intendancy of Coahuila y Tejas. Mexico established the Department of Bexar in San Antonio, with authority over a huge territory which covered all of Central, West, and North Texas.

The Imperial Colonization Law under which the first Austinites arrived specified colonists must be Catholic, so Austin's first three hundred families were affected. The 1824 National Colonization Law and the 1825 Coahuila and Texas State Colonization Law said only that foreigners must be Christian and abide by the laws of the nation, thereby implying they would be members of the established church. This left the door open for Protestant preachers to come to Texas.

The *Handbook of Texas Online* says of the *empresario* system: "Empresarios did not own the land within their grants, nor could they issue titles; the state appointed a land commissioner to give deeds only after one hundred families had been settled. Surveyors laid off leagues and labores along the watercourses and roads, after which colonists could chose vacant tracts. The settlers paid fees to the state, the surveyor, the land commissioner, and the clerk, who wrote the deeds on stamped paper and recorded the payments. Austin's plan to restore his family's well-being by selling land was denied because *empresarios* could not receive fees. The state gave them a bonus of 23,000 acres for each 100 families settled. By 1834, at the virtual end of the empresario system, Austin had settled about 966 families and earned 197,000 acres of bonus land that he could locate where he chose. He could sell the land, but only to those willing to live in Texas."

In 1824, Mexican Federalists had established a constitution, and there was substantial support in Bexar for this new government. Yet, the citizens of Coahuila y Tejas in many ways had little more allegiance to central Mexico than they had to Spain. These independent-minded citizens took on the name of *tejanos*, native-born Mexicans who looked more north than south.

The relationship between the *tejanos* and newly arrived Anglo Americans at first was

congenial, and they worked together well. That was not to last. John L. Davis' *Texans One and All* puts it this way:

> Mexico and Spain had created a society of *tejanos* in Texas that was adaptable and productive. Yet, this frontier culture was no match for the future competition with Anglo Americans, who came from the United States in greater numbers and possessed a better technology in terms of communications and weaponry. Within two years of Mexico's independence from Spain, significant numbers of Anglos were allowed to enter Texas. Once the door was opened, it could not be closed.

Santa Anna, the soldier of the Battle of Medina, overthrew the Federalist government and elevated himself to president. Mexico declared U.S. immigration illegal. Jim Bowie (a knife bears his name), who had married into the wealthy Veramendi family, defeated Mexican forces in the Battle of Concepción, and the forces of Stephen F. Austin took over San Antonio. Such famous *Texians* (a term generally used to apply to a citizen of the Anglo-American sector of the provinces of Coahuila y Tejas or of the Republic of Texas) as Ben Milam led the way in the Siege of Bexar. In December 1835, Martín Perfecto de Cos, the Mexican commander of the city and brother-in-law to Santa Anna, surrendered to the *Texians* in a small residence now known as the Cos House. It is in the La Villita complex at the entrance to the Arneson Theater, on the San Antonio River. This affront to family honor offers another reason why Santa Anna came to San Antonio.

The Mexican president, angered by the activities of the upstarts in Bexar, and bolstered by divisions within the provisional government of the *Texians*, assembled an army of nearly five thousand men and marched north from Mexico City to San Antonio. In San Antonio, famous men of Texas history such as Bowie, William B. Travis, and an adventurous soul from Tennessee named Davy Crockett gathered forces in the Alamo complex to await the arrival of Santa Anna. Bowie and Travis were to have joint command of the forces, but Bowie relinquished his command when he fell ill. As Santa Anna advanced on the Alamo, some of the Anglo settlers who had come to the area fled toward Louisiana, fearing for their lives, in what became known as the "Runaway Scrape." Even after Sam Houston secured Texas' independence, many of them did not return.

Despite the hundreds of books which have been written, and continue to be written, many questions still remain of what happened at the Alamo. Most historians put the *Texian-tejano* force between 180 and 190 people, but others think up to 50 to 60 reinforcements actually may have arrived during the 13 days of the battle—February 13 to March 6, 1836. Regardless of the number of those inside the Alamo complex, all but the wives of two

Above: Antonio Lopez de Santa Anna was the president of Mexico who defeated the Texian-Tejano forces at the Alamo.
COURTESY OF THE INSTITUTE OF TEXAN CULTURES AT THE UNIVERSITY OF TEXAS AT SAN ANTONIO.

Below: The Alamo, Mission San Antonio de Valero, by Theodore Gentilz, shows the ragged roofline of the mission after the battle.
COURTESY OF ST. MARY'S UNIVERSITY AND THE WITTE MUSEUM, SAN ANTONIO, TEXAS.

Left: William Barret Travis commanded the Texian-tejano forces at the Alamo.
COURTESY OF THE INSTITUTE OF TEXAN CULTURES AT THE UNIVERSITY OF TEXAS AT SAN ANTONIO.

Right: James Bowie was one of the defenders of the Alamo.
COURTESY OF THE TEXAS STATE CAPITOL AND THE INSTITUTE OF TEXAN CULTURES AT THE UNIVERSITY OF TEXAS AT SAN ANTONIO.

soldiers, several children, and one African-American slave lost their lives.

The flag which flew above the Alamo was the 1824 flag of the Federalists. This was not a fight between or among ethnic forces. Nor was it a war against the nation of Mexico. It was a fight against Santa Anna, an effort to defeat him so that Mexico could be returned to Federalist control. Toribio Losoya, whose family had lived at the edge of the Alamo compound, was one of the many *tejanos* who died at the Alamo. Another *tejano* who died in the battle was Gregorio Esparza, whose son Enrique was a witness to the battle. Yet, the story is complicated in that those in the Alamo may have learned that leaders had assembled in East Texas on March 2 and declared Texas free from Mexico. The Alamo fell four days after Texas declared itself a free nation. The Battle of the Alamo has gone down in the history books alongside some of the most famous battles ever fought. The sacrifice there brought forth the cry of "Remember the Alamo," giving courage to many future Texans on battlefields across the years.

On the larger scale, the Battle of the Alamo was only one piece in a revolutionary war against Santa Anna which began in Mexico and spread to Texas. In even a larger realm, it is part of an idea that began very early in America, continued through Thomas Jefferson's buying the Louisiana Purchase from the French, and through to "Manifest Destiny." This was the concept that in some way God ordained that the United States should be one nation, from sea to shining sea.

A little more than a month after the fall of the Alamo to Santa Anna, Sam Houston and the Texian forces defeated the Mexican president at San Jacinto, on a peninsula outside current-day Houston, securing the declaration of independence made March 2. In one account, by that time, Juan Seguin, the *tejano* mayor of San Antonio, had collected what he believed to be the ashes of the bones of the heroes of the Alamo. Santa Anna had ordered all the bodies to be burned. Seguin took the ashes to San Fernando Church, where they now rest in a sarcophagus just inside the entrance to San Fernando Cathedral.

At some point along the way toward independence, the name San Antonio de Valero had given way to a nickname—the Alamo. It could have been because many cottonwood trees (*álamo* is the Spanish word for poplar, and the cottonwood is a type of poplar) grew near the mission. Most likely, however, it gained its new name from a company of mounted lancers that had arrived from the Coahuila, Mexico, town of San José y Santiago del Alamo de Parras to help bolster the Spanish militia

Left: The marriage of James Bowie to a daughter of the wealthy Veramendi family of Bexar County is recorded in the 1830s in the records of the Roman Catholic Archdiocese of San Antonio as "Buoy."

Below: The Veramendi Palace on Soledad Street (shown in the 1870s) in San Antonio was the home of one of the wealthiest families in Bexar County.

COURTESY OF THE INSTITUTE OF TEXAN CULTURES AT THE UNIVERSITY OF TEXAS AT SAN ANTONIO.

A William H. Huddle painting of frontiersman-politician David Crockett, one of the defenders of the Alamo.

COURTESY OF THE TEXAS STATE CAPITOL AND THE INSTITUTE OF TEXAN CULTURES AT THE UNIVERSITY OF TEXAS AT SAN ANTONIO.

and the Royal troops of the Bexar presidio in the early 1800s.

One thing we do know is that the Alamo of the early 1800s, up to and after the famous battle fought there, was not the structure we know today. The chapel itself was left unfinished, while other structures in the Alamo complex were built. The chapel did not have a roof until nearly 1850, when the United States Army roofed it and erected the famous curved parapet on the front of the building. Whether the Alamo chapel was used as a church, with only open-air Masses, before the crown secularized the missions in the 1790s is not known, even though the sacristy probably was used as a chapel. It is known that the hundreds of paintings showing the Battle of the Alamo taking place in front of a roofed and parapeted church, and scores of motion pictures showing the same, are not historically correct. The newest Alamo movie, which premiered in March 2004, depicts the correct line of the chapel.

The victory at San Jacinto and the deposition of Santa Anna did not begin to answer the questions of governance. The Republic of Texas was formed, making Texas the only state to have been its own nation, other than Hawaii, before it was a state, but boundary lines and controversies remained quite open. Mexican forces occupied San Antonio at least twice more before the U.S. annexed Texas as a state in 1845. Even after Texas became a state, the squabbling continued. Mexico claimed the Nueces River as the border of Texas, while the United States claimed the Rio Grande. The United States fought a war with Mexico over disputed land rights.

When Texas came into the union, it claimed a territory which spanned not only all of current Texas, but also a huge tract of land spiraling northwest almost to what is now Wyoming. The claim also included more than half the present New Mexico, a third of Colorado, and a corner of Oklahoma. The area had been designated the Department of Bexar by the Spanish. Bexar County by interpolation stretched nearly to Cheyenne, Wyoming. Texas exercised treaties with the United States, Mexico, Spain, and France to arrive at the current easily recognized outline of Texas. Bexar County underwent partitioning into the 1860s to carve it back to its current boundaries. Out of the initial area in current-day Texas, which had been the Department of Bexar, 128 counties were formed.

Texas' congress had created the county government of Bexar on December 22, 1836, making San Antonio the county seat, and it was organized July 3, 1837. Sam Houston, the president of the republic, named Joseph Baker the first chief justice (a title which later became county judge) of Bexar County.

Because Bexar County went through a chaotic time from 1836 to 1848, the population had dropped significantly. In 1844, there were only about one thousand residents, nine-tenths of them of Mexican descent. In less than a decade, the situation changed again. In 1850, the county claimed about fifty-six hundred citizens and almost as many cattle. There was some subsistence farming, with less than five percent of the county land area under cultivation. A major source of revenue became trade carried on by wagon trains to Mexico and New Orleans.

During Santa Anna's incursion into Texas, the *tejanos* had not been well treated. After the Texas Revolution of 1836, the ill treatment continued under the Anglo Americans who had fought alongside some of the key *tejanos* in securing a free Texas. Many native-born Mexicans were driven out of Texas. In addition, the Anglo Americans treated the native-born Mexicans with such distain that many other *tejano* families left for Mexico voluntarily, and the Mexican population of San Antonio began to dwindle significantly.

There were notable exceptions in the stories of prominent *tejanos* remaining in Bexar—José Antonio Navarro was a member of the Texas Congress during the days of the republic and served in the Texas Legislature after statehood, and Francisco Ruiz served as the first Bexar senator to the Texas Congress. Navarro and Ruiz were the only native-born to sign the Texas Declaration of Independence. Juan Seguín (the town of Seguin, in Guadalupe County east of Bexar, was later named for him) fled to Mexico and later fought—probably against his will—for Mexico against the United States in the Mexican War.

For more than sixty years, immigration from Mexico nearly ceased, and Bexar become more Anglo in culture, language and head count. The influx of new Mexican immigrants did not pick up until after the turn of the twentieth century, when revolution and agricultural disaster joined hands to make Mexico a land of chaos and uncertainty. At that point, a new wave of immigration began to change the face of Bexar.

In February 1848, when under the Treaty of Guadalupe Hidalgo, Mexico ceded Texas (setting the boundary as the Rio Grande), California, New Mexico and most of Arizona to the United States, relations became even more strained.

Left: Juan Nepomuceno Seguin was mayor of San Antonio during the Battle of the Alamo. He took the ashes of the Alamo heroes to San Fernando Church.
COURTESY OF THE TEXAS STATE ARCHIVES AND THE INSTITUTE OF TEXAN CULTURES AT THE UNIVERSITY OF TEXAS AT SAN ANTONIO.

Right: Jose Antonio Navarro (from McArdle's notebook, Dawn at the Alamo) *was one of the noted Tejanos.*
COURTESY OF THE ARCHIVES DIVISION, TEXAS STATE LIBRARY.

Chapter III

Courthouses, Travelers, Trails, Tracks

By the middle of the nineteenth century, the county's first courthouse, *Casas Reales*, had seen its day. It had witnessed more than a century of historical development, including the use of the whipping post and an 1840 battle, the Council House fight, between representatives of the Texas government and the Comanche Nation. Construction of the county's second courthouse and jail began September 6, 1850, on a site on *Plaza de Armas* (Military Plaza), a block west of the *Casas Reales*. The new courthouse housed county facilities, including a second-floor district courtroom and all courthouse functions. It also included the city offices, signaling an historically close relationship between county and city government in Bexar, a factor most important in the area's development nearly 150 years later. A separate building housed the jail.

The main building, known as the "Bat Cave" because of a large colony of bats roosting in the roof structure that often disrupted governmental business, continued as a county and city governmental complex until 1889. Then it was demolished to make way for a new City Hall, the San Antonio City Hall still in use. Even though the Bat Cave remained a county-city site for nearly forty years, there were discussions long and often as to its adequacy to serve the county. As early as March 1857, plans began for a new three-story courthouse, to be built at Travis and Soledad, two blocks to the northeast, but the building never came into existence. The Civil War got in the way.

After the war and during Reconstruction, talk of a new county courthouse once again began. The city was using part of the French Building, which had been built between 1856 and 1858 on Dwyer Avenue immediately east of the current Bexar County Courthouse as the most modern structure in San Antonio of the antebellum period. It had served as the Confederate headquarters during the war, and county fathers had their eye on the fine building. In April 1868 they declared the French Building the county's new courthouse, but kept the district court "where it is," presumably the Bat Cave.

Less than four years later, in February 1872, the county and city broke all governmental ranks, and the city took full possession of the Bat Cave. The county again was in the market for a new courthouse, but the city leaders gave the county a while to find a new structure. Alamo Lodge No. 44 A.F. and A.M., the oldest Masonic Lodge in Texas, had been unable to service its debt on its three-story building on Soledad a few blocks north of the French Building. The county agreed to pay the indebtedness and took over the building in October 1872.

The Masonic Building was expanded in 1874. In 1881, county officials, spurred both by the lack of space in the county building and emboldened by powers the 1876 Texas Constitution had given them under a commission form of government, decided to expand the structure again. They offered a $100 prize to an architect furnishing the best plan to renovate the Masonic Building. Alfred Giles, an Englishman who became quite famous as the designer of numerous public buildings and homes in Bexar, won the prize. His plan doubled the size of the Masonic Building and transformed it into an imposing Second Empire structure topped by a mansard roof. In 1883, on accepting the renovated building as the courthouse, commissioners commended Giles and the contractor, D. C. Anderson, for the new $40,000 project.

In 1877, Giles had won the contract to design a new county jail separate from the courthouse. In October 1878 the commissioners accepted the new structure, built on Cameron Street a block north of City Hall for $13,037, by contractor Edward Walsh. The limestone structure, with a two-story façade and atrium, appeared quite castle-like. It housed the old wooden scaffold used as the gallows. In 1911, a remodeling by Henry T. Phelps added two floors, doing away with the atrium and installing a trap door between the second and first floor to be part of the gallows. He also added Spanish-like bell towers. In 1926 the county expanded the building to five floors, as designed by

Opposite: Carl Hilmar Guenther built a famous flour mill on the San Antonio River.

COURTESY OF THE PIONEER FLOUR MILLS AND THE INSTITUTE OF TEXAN CULTURES AT THE UNIVERSITY OF TEXAS AT SAN ANTONIO.

Above: The "Bat Cave" on Military Plaza, Bexar County's second courthouse, also housed City Hall and the jail. Copied from a stereograph by Alexis V. Latourette.
COURTESY OF THE SAN ANTONIO CONSERVATION SOCIETY AND THE INSTITUTE OF TEXAN CULTURES AT THE UNIVERSITY OF TEXAS AT SAN ANTONIO.

Below: Another view of the "Bat Cave," in 1850, highlighting the jail.
COURTESY OF THE GRANDJEAN COLLECTION OF THE DAUGHTERS OF THE REPUBLIC OF TEXAS LIBRARY AT THE ALAMO AND THE BEXAR COUNTY SHERIFFS OFFICE.

Atlee B. Ayres. The county used the 1878 jail structure until 1962, when it built a new jail elsewhere. This 1878 jail was the site of the last hanging by the county in February 1923. After this time, the state took over all executions and used the electric chair.

The accolades bestowed on Giles for the restored Masonic Building were short-lived. The new design developed cracks, and Giles was placed on the hot seat about building safety. The county rented space in the Kampmann Building at Commerce and Soledad to help relieve stress on the Masonic Building.

In February 1887, commissioners again resolved a new courthouse was in order, to be constructed on the Masonic Building site. Architect James Murphy drew plans, but the building he designed was not built. The commissioners, noting a rise in county population from about 30,500 in 1880 to near 50,000 by 1890, launched another round of talks to build yet another building, this time on a different site. That building was to become the Bexar County Courthouse still in use today. It was designed by James Riely Gordon.

In the nineteenth century, waves of immigration changed the faces (and face) of Bexar County residents. Economic and political unrest in Germany was sending a steady stream of citizens to Central Texas. Some formed small German towns, where some still speak German. They founded Adelsverein, a society of German nobles, in New Braunfels and Fredericksburg. Others moved into San Antonio, opening mercantile establishments. Many of the German immigrants first settled in La Villita, then moved to a more upscale area a short distance away named for a Prussian king, Wilhelm I. On King William Street and surrounding areas, they built fine homes in an area which once had been the farmlands of the Alamo. During the anti-German hysteria of World War I, the area was renamed for General John J. Pershing, head of the Allied Expeditionary Force. It was changed back to King William Street in the 1920s. Today it is one of the most-popular historic attractions in San Antonio and the first residential neighborhood named a historic district in the U.S.

Among the most prominent of the German merchants in the makers of San Antonio was Eduard Steves, who came to Texas in 1849, settling first in New Braunfels and then in Comfort, before coming to San Antonio in 1866. He established a lumber company now

Above: *The French Building, on Plaza de las Islas and Dwyer, was used as a county courthouse.*

COURTESY OF MARY ANN GUERRA, WANDITA FORD TURNER, AND THE INSTITUTE OF TEXAN CULTURES AT THE UNIVERSITY OF TEXAS AT SAN ANTONIO.

Below: *The Masonic Hall was used as one of the Bexar County courthouses.*

COURTESY OF THOMAS W. CUTRER AND THE INSTITUTE OF TEXAN CULTURES AT THE UNIVERSITY OF TEXAS AT SAN ANTONIO.

operated by the fifth generation in the family, with the holdings including one of the largest door companies in the world. The Steves Homestead in the King William district was a family-owned home until 1952, when it was donated to the San Antonio Conservation Society as a museum. Eduard Steves' descendants continue to comprise one of the most active families working for civic improvement in Bexar County. The King William District also is the location of a flour mill built in the late 1850s by Carl Hilmar Guenther. He came from Germany to the United States in 1848 and built a mill in Fredericksburg in the Texas Hill Country before moving his family to San Antonio. Today, Pioneer Flour Mills is one of the best-known businesses in Bexar County. By 1876, Germans made up one third of the population and furnished leaders in politics, business, culture, education, and social affairs.

The Institute of Texan Cultures, part of the University of Texas at San Antonio, identifies more than two dozen distinct ethnic groups which have settled in Texas. Many of these groups have been, and continue to be, represented in Bexar. Some of the most prominent families in the community have come from other nations and intermarried to form a hardy stock of citizenry. In family trees of such well-known Bexar pioneer families as Steves, Frost, Tobin, and Maverick, one will find the names of Canary Islanders, for instance. The Institute hosts the Texas Folklife Festival each year in celebration of the cultural diversity of the state. Next to Fiesta San Antonio, it is the most popular festival of the year.

The Anglo Americans who came with the Austins to Texas from such states as Missouri

Above: The Cameron Street Jail, c. 1900.
COURTESY OF THE SAN ANTONIO CONSERVATION SOCIETY AND THE BEXAR COUNTY SHERIFFS OFFICE.

Below: The Cameron Street Jail, c. 1925, after it was expanded.
PHOTOGRAPH BY ATLEE B. AYRES. COURTESY OF THE INSTITUTE OF TEXAN CULTURES AT THE UNIVERSITY OF TEXAS AT SAN ANTONIO.

and Tennessee were not a uniform group. They included representatives of English, Scottish, Welsh, Irish, Dutch, Danish, and German origin. Even those called "English" were a mixture of Nordic-Germanic-Celtic stock. Included in those of mostly English descent coming to Bexar in the mid-1860s was Thomas Claiborne Frost, who arrived in Texas from Alabama in 1854. He had been a Latin teacher in college, a law student under the tutelage of the legal counsel to Sam Houston, a colonel in the Confederacy, and a Texas Ranger. He began the operation of a horse-and-wagon freight line between San Antonio and Indianola and went into the mercantile business in the Alamo City. He launched a banking business, dating Frost National Bank to 1868. Today that family-owned bank remains one of the largest, best known and most respected financial institutions in the Southwest.

The Hungarians never were a large part of Bexar society, but some did become well known in their time in San Antonio. Laslo Ujhazi, or Uhjazzi, or Ujhazy, who had been a civil governor of the Komarom fortress in the ill-fated 1848 Hungarian revolution against Austrian rule, came to Bexar and formed Texas' first small Hungarian center. His daughter, Helen Madarasz, was the first Hungarian businesswoman in Texas and founded with her son, Ladislaus, a nursery in the area that now is part of Brackenridge Park and the San Antonio Zoological Gardens. Alois Goebel and his daughters were celebrated public musicians in San Antonio, and the family of Ludwig Varga became well known in saddle making.

Eleven Irishmen died at the Alamo and one-seventh of Sam Houston's army at San Jacinto was Irish. Even though the Irish did establish a neighborhood on the near eastern edge of downtown San Antonio, most of the houses often called "the Irish flat" in the Alamo City are no longer standing. John Twohig was an early land developer and philanthropist. Among Irish Texans, one of the best-known was Margaret Mary Healy Murphy, who founded the first religious order in Texas to educate African-American children. She opened the Peter Claver School in San Antonio. It is now the Healy Murphy Center for educating school dropouts, directed enthusiastically in more recent years by the late Sister Mary Boniface O'Neill. San Antonio still has several Irish organizations, including the Irish Cultural Society and the Harp and Shamrock Society. One of the best known paintings of Texas history is *Dawn at the Alamo*, which hangs in the state capitol. It is by Irishman Harry Arthur McArdle.

During the Spanish colonial days, African Americans had lived in Bexar and were involved

Left: *The Cameron Street Jail, June 16, 1938, after another expansion.*
COURTESY OF THE SAN ANTONIO LIGHT COLLECTION, THE INSTITUTE OF TEXAN CULTURES AT THE UNIVERSITY OF TEXAS AT SAN ANTONIO AND THE BEXAR COUNTY SHERIFF'S OFFICE.

Below: *The Kampmann Building, at Soledad and Commerce, was yet another Bexar County courthouse. Shown here on November 14, 1939, the building later was demolished.*
COURTESY OF THE SAN ANTONIO LIGHT COLLECTION, THE INSTITUTE OF TEXAN CULTURES AT THE UNIVERSITY OF TEXAS AT SAN ANTONIO.

Above: The Steves Lumber Co., at Walnut and Fifth, was an early San Antonio business. It is shown here in 1881.

COURTESY OF THE SAN ANTONIO LIGHT COLLECTION, THE INSTITUTE OF TEXAN CULTURES AT THE UNIVERSITY OF TEXAS AT SAN ANTONIO.

Right: The late Johanna Kloepper Steves is seated in front of the Steves Homestead in the King William District.

COURTESY OF THE SAN ANTONIO CONSERVATION SOCIETY AND THE INSTITUTE OF TEXAN CULTURES AT THE UNIVERSITY OF TEXAS AT SAN ANTONIO.

in farming, blacksmithing, teaching, and selling. The Spanish accepted inter-marriage and individual accomplishment without denying the necessity of slavery. Yet, there always was understated discrimination against those of mixed blood. From 1836 to the end of the Civil War, although the African-American population of Bexar could be vulnerable to enslavement, many chose to remain, including free African Americans such as Hendrick Arnold. After the war, the county's population increased dramatically, and by 1880 was nearly four thousand, three times what it had been before the war. Many of the freed slaves sought out work as a cowboy or joined the military. After the war, all or part of three African-American regiments were stationed in San Antonio, and they were involved in more than half the engagements against hostile Indians in Texas. At one point in 1867, more than eight hundred African-American troops of the Ninth Cavalry Regiment were in training at San Pedro Springs. They were among the troops on the frontier who were called the "Buffalo Soldiers" by the Native Americans.

Even though discrimination against both African Americans and Hispanics certainly has not been conquered in Bexar County or anywhere else, desegregation of facilities in the area came about quite peaceably in the two decades following World War II. One of those African-American leaders who worked to bring about this development was the Reverend Claude Black, the minister of Mt. Zion Second Baptist Church. Today this population of San Antonio is involved actively in civic ventures and contributes to the cultural life of the county. For most of the last century, much of the African-American population of the area became concentrated in the eastern sector of the county, just south of Fort Sam Houston. Today expanded opportunities have led to a more random and county-wide African-American presence.

The Polish who came to Texas remained primarily rural, some settling in East Bexar County. Father Leopold Mocygemba, a Polish Franciscan missionary working out of New Braunfels, influenced families from Upper Silesia to move to Texas. On Christmas Eve 1854, the group founded Panna Maria in Karnes County south of San Antonio. It is the oldest permanent Polish colony in the United States and the home of the nation's first Polish Catholic Church and school. A Polish soldier in the Texas army, known to history only as "Private Kaminski," died in the Council House fight at Casas Reales in San Antonio in 1840. A Polish newspaper, *Nowiny Texaskie* (*Texas News*) was published in San Antonio from 1913 to 1920.

Some Polish immigrants formed the rural community of St. Hedwig. Others settled in the "Polish Quarter" of San Antonio, which was located in the area that was razed for HemisFair. The Tower of the Americas was constructed close to the previous location of St. Michael's Church.

The graves of members of the Steves family in City Cemetery No. 1.

Chapter III ✦ 31

The Italian presence in Bexar never was large but some of the Italians who served the community made important names for themselves. Giuseppe Cassini, known as José Cassiano, provided food to rebelling *Texians* from his San Antonio store. He fled the Alamo City, but later returned as a major landowner. Pompeo Coppini sculpted many important works in San Antonio, including friezes on downtown buildings and statues, and an art institute in San Antonio still bears his name. Among his most-famous works is the Alamo Cenotaph, erected to commemorate the Texas Centennial in 1936. The Lucchese family made its name in bootmaking and one Lucchese daughter, Josephine, was an internationally known coloratura soprano.

The Greek presence in Bexar has not been large but the community gleefully enjoys an annual fall Greek festival, Funstival, at St. Sophia Greek Orthodox Church. The Garden Fruit Store of Elias "Pappa Louis" Varessis long was a favorite shopping spot for San Antonians.

The Japanese population was best identified prior to World War II with the Japanese Tea Garden in a huge rock quarry at the edge of Brackenridge Park. During the 1930s, the Kimi Jingi family lived in the garden, but the family was forced to leave with the outbreak of war, and the garden was renamed the Chinese Tea Garden by citizens suspicious of the Japanese. In later years, the city renamed the area to honor the Japanese founder. Some of the Japanese-American citizens who had been interned in federal camps in South Texas during the war remained in Texas following hostilities, and

some came to Bexar. Also, "war brides" from Japan increased the Japanese population in the Alamo City.

The story of the Chinese in Texas and Bexar is quite different. In earlier days, the Chinese arrived primarily as railroad workers, but the largest contingent came as "Pershing's Chinese." In the late years of the nineteenth century, federal legislation excluded the Chinese from immigrating to the United States. In 1917,

Opposite, top: In the late 1840s, Dia de San Juan, the Corrida de la Sandia was popular in Bexar County. The game, a competitive watermelon race, was akin to basketball on horseback. From a painting by Theodore Gentilz.
COURTESY OF THE TORCH COLLECTION, HOUSTON, TEXAS.

Opposite, bottom: The Frost & Bro. store on Plaza de las Islas was the forerunner to Frost National Bank.
COURTESY OF TOM FROST, FROST NATIONAL BANK.

Top, left: Helen Madarasz was the first Hungarian businesswoman in Texas, c. 1890. She established the first nursery in the area on land which now is the San Antonio Zoo and Brackenridge Park.
COURTESY OF PETER BOGATI AND THE INSTITUTE OF TEXAN CULTURES AT THE UNIVERSITY OF TEXAS AT SAN ANTONIO.

Top, right: Margaret Mary Healy Murphy, in a photograph by H. R. Marks, Austin, c. 1870s, was the founder of the Healy Murphy School for black children in San Antonio.
COURTESY OF THE CONVENT OF THE HOLY GHOST AND MARY IMMACULATE AND THE INSTITUTE OF TEXAN CULTURES AT THE UNIVERSITY OF TEXAS AT SAN ANTONIO.

Left: Alois Goebel (in rear) and his musical group played at the Menger Hotel. With him are Helen C. Behnke (left), and his daughters, Antonio Goebel Cornelius, Marianne Goebel Banspach, and Virginain Goebel Marrs.
COURTESY OF BERNICE CASEY AND THE INSTITUTE OF TEXAN CULTURES AT THE UNIVERSITY OF TEXAS AT SAN ANTONIO.

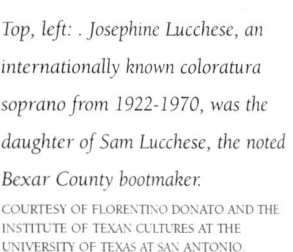

Top, left: . Josephine Lucchese, an internationally known coloratura soprano from 1922-1970, was the daughter of Sam Lucchese, the noted Bexar County bootmaker.

COURTESY OF FLORENTINO DONATO AND THE INSTITUTE OF TEXAN CULTURES AT THE UNIVERSITY OF TEXAS AT SAN ANTONIO.

Top, right: Coppini's cenotaph on Alamo Plaza, commemorating the hundredth anniversary of the independence of Texas.

Below: A celebration of the Asian Festival on January 10, 2003.

COURTESY OF THE INSTITUTE OF TEXAN CULTURES AT THE UNIVERSITY OF TEXAS AT SAN ANTONIO.

General John J. Pershing sponsored a notable exception to the exclusion. In his unsuccessful efforts in Mexico in an attempt to arrest the illusive Francisco "Pancho" Villa, Pershing had the aid of Chinese families in northern Mexico. They provided food and supplies. In return, Pershing allowed five hundred families to follow him out of Mexico, and the U.S. government gave the Chinese permission to stay in Texas. A settlement of four hundred Chinese families in Bexar County formed the first Chinese community in Texas. The family-oriented Chinese placed a high premium on education, establishing Chinese schools as early as 1922. Mary Eng started the first Chinese school in San Antonio.

Although only about one percent of the population was Asian in the 2000 census, the Asian community is quite culturally and ethnically diverse. Each year, fourteen Asian ethnic groups gather at the Institute of Texan Cultures to celebrate an Asian Festival, under the leadership of Evelyn Crow (Filipino), Mary Lam (Chinese), and Rene'e Park (Hawaiian-Korean). The festival was founded in 1985 by Lam at the San Antonio Museum of Art, moving to the Institute in 2000. Of the Asian community, about six thousand Iranians are listed in the population. May Lam provided a listing of some of the most prominent Asian leaders in Bexar County over the years. The list includes Dr. Rajam Ramamurthy, the first woman president of the Bexar County Medical Society; the late City Councilman Frank Wing; Dr. P. M. Ku, who headed aeronautical and lubrication facilities at Southwest Research Institute; Dr. Wen-Hwa Lee, former director of The Institute of Biotechnology at the Texas Research Park; Edward Mok, founder of the

Marmon Mok archi-tectural firm, and Clifford Hew and Elisa Chan, structural engineers for major highway projects in Texas.

One of the major increases in the Asian population in the community came in the 1980s, due to the relaxation of immigration laws passed in 1965 and Indochinese refugees from the Vietnam War. Families from Vietnam, Laos and Cambodia settled in San Antonio. Many Korean brides had also arrived as a result of the Korean War and subsequent U.S. major troop deployments to South Korea.

The most-notable citizen of Holland to have lived in Texas was Phillip Hendrick Nering Bogel, who took on the name of Felipe Enrique Neri, Baron de Bastrop, claiming aristocracy. He came to San Antonio about 1810, was elected to a high municipal governmental position and established a reputation that today would label him a "wheeler dealer." He had befriended Moses Austin and was the person responsible for the Spanish government eventually approving Austin's petition to colonize in Texas. The baron became commissioner of colonization for the Austin movement and a member of the Mexican legislature in Texas. "If Stephen F. Austin is the 'father of Anglo Texas,'" wrote John L. Davis, "the Dutch con man Bogel is certainly the godfather."

Already it has been pointed out that the Frenchman La Salle had a significant effect on the development of the area. Not until 1844 did the French make significant inroads into the Bexar area. Henri Castro, an adventurous French banker, founded the town of Castroville just outside today's southwest boundary of Bexar, and brought two thousand Alsatians to settle. Today, Castroville's St. Louis Day celebration, sponsored by the St. Louis Catholic Church, is a favorite outing each August for thousands of San Antonians.

In 1848, Francois Giraud, a South Carolinian of French parentage, studied metallurgical engineering in France and then became a county surveyor. In 1854, he convinced city leaders to set aside San Pedro Springs as a park. San Pedro is considered the second oldest city park in the United States, second only to Boston Commons. New York City's Central Park, also developed during the 1850s, was the first landscaped public park in the nation. Giraud

Above: Kimo Eizo, Jr. (left), Mabel Yoshiko, Rae Sayoko, Ruth Emiko, and Miyoshi Jingu greet guests at the Japanese Tea Garden in Brackenridge Park on February 11, 1937.

COURTESY OF THE SAN ANTONIO LIGHT COLLECTION, THE INSTITUTE OF TEXAN CULTURES AT THE UNIVERSITY OF TEXAS AT SAN ANTONIO.

Left: In the early twenty-first century, the Japanese Tea Garden in Brackenridge Park was in disrepair.

Above: An expedition, including those known as "Pershing's Chinese," leave Mexico on January 28, 1917.
COURTESY OF THE LIBRARY OF CONGRESS AND THE INSTITUTE OF TEXAN CULTURES AT THE UNIVERSITY OF TEXAS AT SAN ANTONIO.

Right: Bexar County Belgian farmers in 1908 have their vegetables prepared for market. They are Prosper Versaet (left); his wife, Emma; Delphina Bauwens; Aviel Bauwens (Delphina's son); and Aviel's wife, Mary.
COURTESY OF MRS. HOMER VERSTUYFT AND THE INSTITUTE OF TEXAN CULTURES AT THE UNIVERSITY OF TEXAS AT SAN ANTONIO.

redefined the boundaries and structures of the missions and designed the buildings for the Ursuline Academy and the original buildings of St. Mary's Institute and the French Gothic cathedral of San Fernando. This new cathedral, incorporating the structure of the Spanish Colonial church, was opened in 1873, when Giraud was mayor of San Antonio. In 2003 an $18-million renovation of the cathedral was completed in an attempt to restore some of the charm which Giraud had built into the structure and add new points of structure for worship.

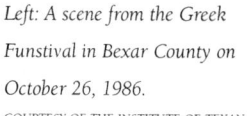

Left: A scene from the Greek Funstival in Bexar County on October 26, 1986.
COURTESY OF THE INSTITUTE OF TEXAN CULTURES AT THE UNIVERSITY OF TEXAS AT SAN ANTONIO.

Below: The Garden Fruit Store, owned by Elias "Pappa Louis" Varessis, was a popular Bexar County shopping place.
COURTESY OF ELIAS VARESSIS AND THE INSTITUTE OF TEXAN CULTURES AT THE UNIVERSITY OF TEXAS AT SAN ANTONIO.

A new City Centre museum has opened next door to the cathedral, with a community center nearby.

The first historical notation of a citizen from Belgium in Bexar was made in 1719, when Juan Banual, a blacksmith, arrived in the area. He did much of the ironwork at Mission San José and Mission San Antonio de Valero (the Alamo), where he and his wife once lived and where he operated the smithy shop and sawmill. In the 1850s, a Belgian stonemason, Theodore Vander Straten, helped the U.S. Army repair falling Alamo walls, just about the time one of his kinsman, Anton Diedrick, was renamed "Anton

Cattle drives from the mid-1860s until the early 1890s were important to the economy of Bexar County. This is an engraving by A.R. Waud, A Drove of Cattle Crossing a Stream, *from Harper's Weekly, October 19, 1867.*

COURTESY OF THE INSTITUTE OF TEXAN CULTURES AT THE UNIVERSITY OF TEXAS AT SAN ANTONIO.

Dutchallover" by an Army that couldn't understand Diedrick's pronunciation of his name in Flemish. "He's Dutch all over, so we will call him that," it was declared. Dutchallover dropped the "all" from the middle of his name when he began to ride as a wagon shotgunner. Still another kinsman was Jean-Charles Houzeau, an astronomer and abolitionist who helped unionists escape San Antonio during the Civil War. He fled but made a trip back to the Alamo City in 1882, to find a vantage point to see Venus cross the sun.

It was as outstanding vegetable farmers that the Belgians won praise in San Antonio. They came to Bexar in 1867, fleeing Mexico after the fall of the government of Maximilian, who had been made emperor by the French. Maximilian's wife, the Empress Carlota, was Belgian, and a substantial number of her countrymen had gone to Mexico with her. Expansive vegetable gardens in west Bexar County, near the later Kelly Air Force Base, and in areas just south, became the domain of the Belgians. Names such as Van de Walle, van Daele, Persyn, Verstuft, and Baten became well known to shoppers in Bexar County. They thanked the Belgian farmers not only for common crops, but also for introducing such specialties as kohlrabi and cauliflower. Today, a few of the fine Belgian farms still operate in south Bexar County, but the glory days of the extensive vegetable gardens are gone.

Inhabitants of Syria and Lebanon did arrive in Bexar but not in large numbers. The ones who did, however, have made strong marks on the community. Solomon and George Casseb were grocers in 1915 and established San Antonio's first supermarket in 1923. Joseph Curry invented and manufactured machinery used in the processing of Mexican food. His brother, Peter Michael Curry, served from 1967 to 1992 as the district judge with the longest tenure in the history of the county. Their sister married Ralph Karam who founded Karam's Restaurant.

While vegetable farming has always been important, cattle ranching was king in the early days of Bexar County. Long-haired Retinto, or Criollo, stock had dropped off Spanish ships on the Texas coast in the 1700s. They had traveled as far as Bexar. When the English cattle brought in by the Anglo Americans met up with the Spanish cattle, the new cattle became known as the Texas Longhorn. The missions owned thousands of animals in well-managed herds.

Bexar had recorded cattle brands as early as the 1740s, and up to ten thousand beeves from Spanish land grant ranches in south Bexar County had been driven up *El Camino Real* into Louisiana in the late 1770s and early

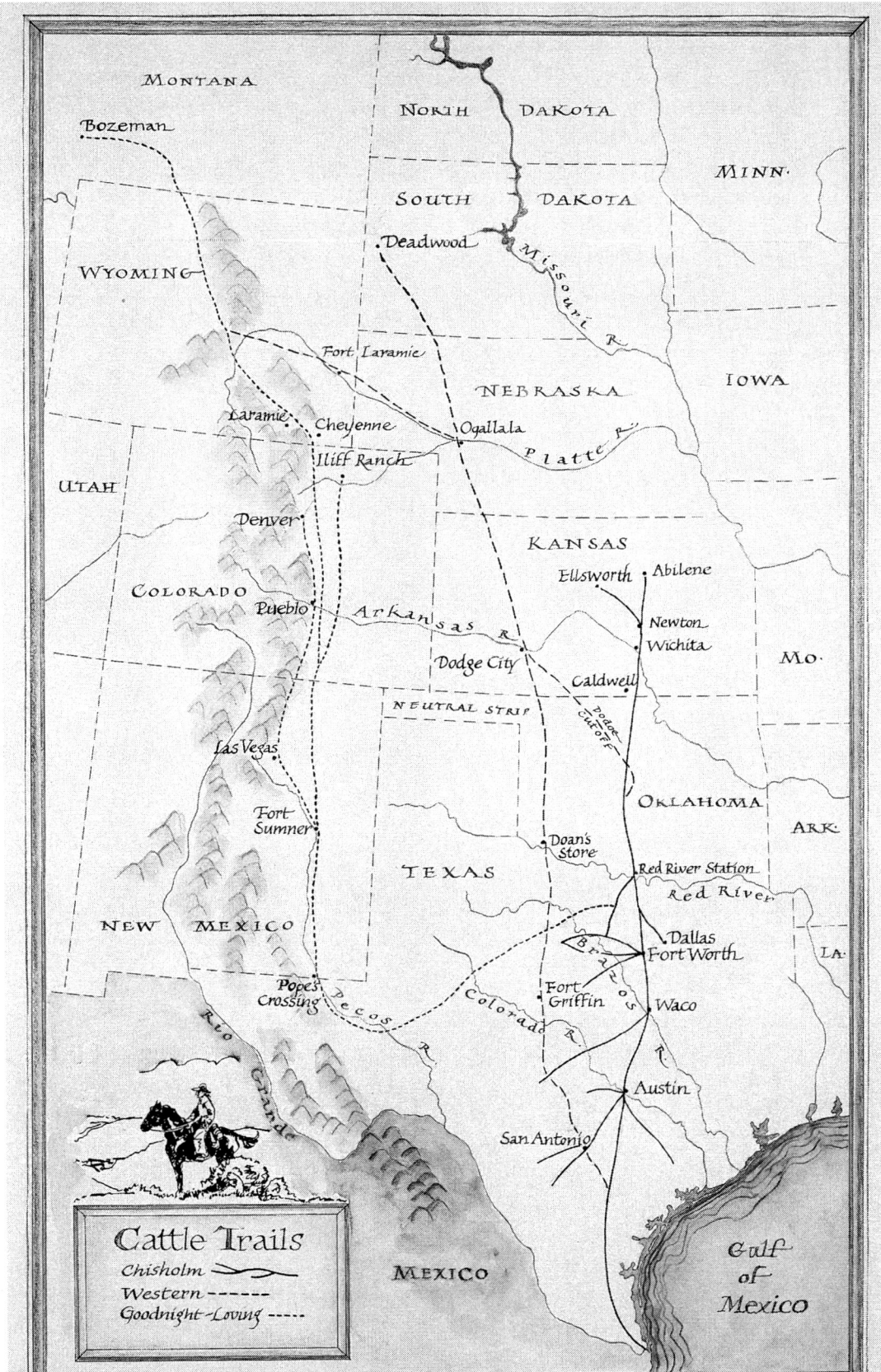

Two of the three major cattle trails, the Western and the Chisholm, went through Bexar County.
MAP BY BARBARA WHITEHEAD. COURTESY OF THE SOUTHWESTERN WRITERS COLLECTION, SAN MARCOS, TEXAS.

1780s. They were to provide meat for the Spanish troops, under the command of Bernardo de Gálvez, who were fighting the British on behalf of the American colonies. Thus, Bexar County was involved in the cattle drive one hundred years before the great cattle drives which enriched American history from 1865 to 1895.

Below: This sculpture in front of Pioneer Hall in San Antonio commemorates the bravery of those who drove ten million head of cattle from Texas during the great trail rides.

Opposite, left: Samuel A. Maverick, from whose name the "maverick," or unbranded cattle, derives, was a chief justice (county judge) of Bexar County and mayor of San Antonio.
COURTESY OF THE INSTITUTE OF TEXAN CULTURES AT THE UNIVERSITY OF TEXAS AT SAN ANTONIO.

Opposite, right: The graves of Samuel Maverick and his wife are in City Cemetery No. 1.

As the Spanish presidial soldiers were the first permanent military presence in Bexar, so the area's *vaqueros* were the first cowpunchers, the forerunner to the American cowboy. Most historians list the cattle brand issued to Juan Joseph (José) Flores by the area's Spanish governor on July 1, 1762, as the first legitimate brand in Bexar. Yet, other brands recorded in the Bexar Archives pre-date this brand. One was issued to Nicolás Saenz on October 4, 1742, and the other to Francisco Joseph de Estrada on January 16, 1748. As the first was issued to a non-resident by a non-resident governor, it may not qualify as the first. Even though the second was issued in the name of several locations, including "this of San Antonio," it may not qualify because its elderly owner really never did go into the cattle business in a major way. Early Mission Espada also had a brand.

Bexar County was at the apex of the diamond-shaped area that was the original Texas cattle kingdom, making it an important center for the ranching industry. From 1860 to 1870 xthe number of beef cattle in the county doubled to more than fifty-five thousand head. Bexar was on the Western Trail and at the edge of the Chisholm Trail. In the years of the great cattle drives, more than ten million head of cattle were driven from Texas, where the price might be $2 a head, to northern points, where a healthy cow might bring $40. The story of the drives can be seen vividly in the Texas Pioneers, Trail Drivers', and Rangers Museum, located next to the Witte Museum, on Broadway close to downtown San Antonio.

There sometimes was a question of the route of the most-famous of the trails, the Chisholm. C. H. Rust, however, leaves no doubt as he relates his trail experiences in J. Marvin Hunter's *The Trail Drivers of Texas*. The Chisholm, he remembered, went from San Antonio to Abilene, Kansas. Another remembrance in the same book tells of how, in 1888, George Saunders, organizer of the Old Trail Drivers' Association, bought a 2,200-pound prize steer called *Joe Bailey* at auction at the Fort Worth Stock Yards for 15 cents a pound, raffled him off, then won him back, then had him slaughtered at the San Antonio yards. He gave most of the beef to state officials, then sold the leftovers for $300.

One of the ironic elements of the cattle business in Texas is that the name perhaps best known around the world as relating to Texas

cattle is that of Samuel A. Maverick, whose name went into the dictionary as being synonymous with unbranded cattle as well as with independent thinkers. Maverick was never a major cattleman by Texas standards. His unbranded cattle wandered from their home on Matagorda Island onto the mainland and went into the history books. Maverick was a signer of the Texas Declaration of Independence, delegate to the Texas Secession Convention, a mayor of San Antonio, and a Bexar County chief justice. He was one of three men to have served as mayor of San Antonio and the county's chief officer. Maverick is buried in City Cemetery No. 1 on San Antonio's East Side. His descendants continue to be among the leading citizens of the Alamo City. One, Maury Maverick, was a noted New Deal congressman and San Antonio mayor whose administration developed the San Antonio River in the city's central business area. The late Maury Maverick, Jr., his son, was a noted civil rights lawyer and political journalist.

A major factor in the economic development of Bexar unfolded on February 2, 1877, when the Galveston, Harrisburg, and San Antonio Railway belched into town as the community's first railroad. Before this, freight had been carried by Mexican *carreta*, large single-axled wagons with massive wheels, pulled by two oxen. Another way was by Prairie Schooner, huge two-axled wagons covered with canvas, pulled by two horses or mules. Most San Antonio trade was with Mexico. For passengers,

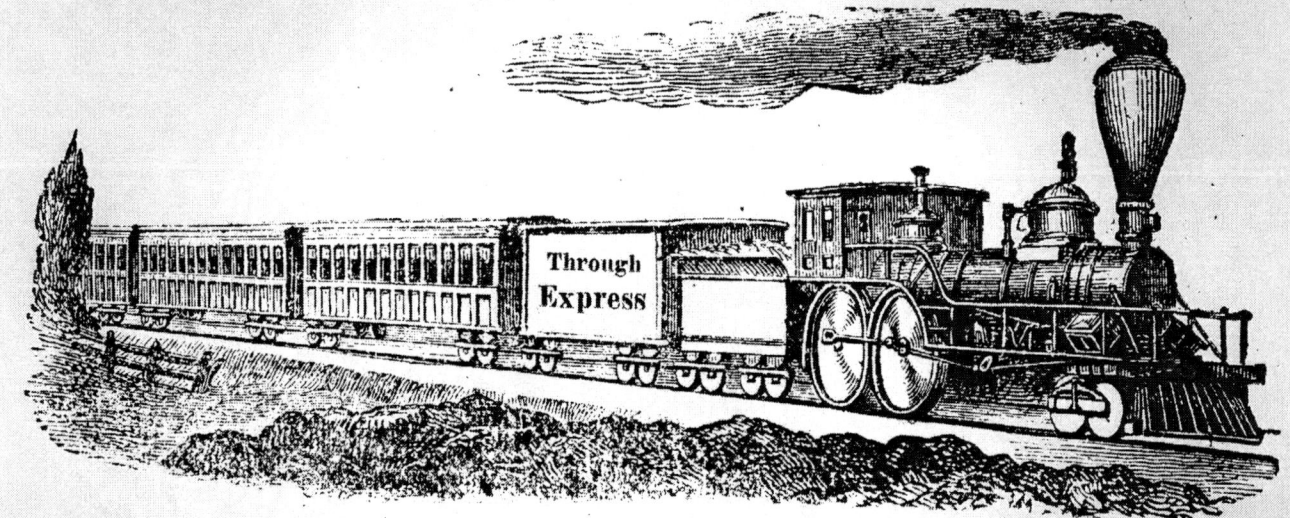

Above: This advertisement heralded the arrival of the railroad in Bexar County in 1877.
COURTESY OF THE INSTITUTE OF TEXAN CULTURES AT THE UNIVERSITY OF TEXAS AT SAN ANTONIO.

Right: The Flores Street and San Pedro Avenue mule-drawn streetcar is in operation in the 1880s.
COURTESY OF THE INSTITUTE OF TEXAN CULTURES AT THE UNIVERSITY OF TEXAS AT SAN ANTONIO.

a stagecoach left for Austin three times a week during the legislative sessions and another went to Indianola, via Seguin, Gonzales, Cuero, and Victoria, with a connection via boat at Indianola to travel to Galveston or New Orleans.

In 1881, the second railroad, the International-Great Northern, arrived, coming from the northeast. In 1883 the first train from San Francisco came, on a line built by the Southern Pacific. In 1884 the San Antonio & Aransas Pass Railroad (SA&AP) was formed, with general offices in San Antonio. A depot was built at South Flores and Aransas Streets, which is now an extension of South Alamo Street. Also, Louis S. Berg, a San Antonio promoter, built a wool-washing mill and a store near Mission San Juan Capistrano to serve the adjacent Berg's Mill community of two hundred residents. The prosperous community opened the Mill Railroad and Platform as early as 1885, which served as a stopping point for the SA&AP. The SA&AP made its trial run to and from Floresville in 1885, and the next year reached Corpus Christi, bringing the Gulf Coast closer than Galveston and creating a flurry of economic activity in the Rio Grande Valley. By 1887 the SA&AP was running three passenger trains and up to six freight trains a day into and out of San Antonio. That year, the inaugural public train to Boerne, 31 miles, demanded a fare of 95 cents and took two hours. Together, the rail lines helped change the physical face of Bexar. New products could come in and go out of the area with much greater ease. Within the city, rail service had an impact also. In 1874 the San Antonio Street Railway Company was organized, and on June 22 the first mule-drawn streetcar began service, from San Pedro Springs to Alamo Plaza.

The railroad made possible the development of the Union Stockyards, which opened between 1889 and 1892. Up to a million cattle a year moved out of the yards during its heyday. At its zenith, more than 70 meat processing plants operated out of the 35-acre stockyards area. Today, there are only two. The Kiolbassa Provision Company, formed in 1949, is in its fifth generation of aggressive family management and is one of the largest regional sausage manufacturers in the state. Perhaps because of the proximity of the stockyard area to the western edge of the downtown area, with new neighborhoods being developed all around, the importance of carrying cattle by rail waned. The last trainload of cattle left the stockyards in 1972, with trucking and other modes taking over. The stockyards closed in April 2001, and the area now supports nearly seventy businesses in an industrial park.

The famous steer still stands above the Union Stock Yards, but he has no more cattle to rule.

CHAPTER IV

GENERALS, TEACHERS, AND PREACHERS

THE MILITARY

The military always has been a friend to Bexar County. After all, part of the plan for control of the area in the early 18th century by the Spanish included the development of the presidio. During Spanish, Mexican and Texan rule, the presence of troops was an important element in the community because it was a frontier area.

The U.S. Army arrived in Bexar in October 1845 to establish a Post at San Antonio, not quite eight months after Texas was admitted to the Union. As early as August 1846, Bexar became an assembly point for the forces of General John E. Wool, fighting in the Mexican War. Serving on Wool's staff was Captain Robert E. Lee. An area designated as Camp Almus, near the Alamo, had been established, and Wool began an effort to consolidate supplies in the Alamo compound. The Alamo chapel itself could not be used, as it was in ruins and had no roof. Also, there was a dispute over who held title to the building, the city or the church. When the settlement ultimately went to the church, the Army in January 1849 leased the Alamo property from the bishop for $150 a month. It leased adjacent grounds from Samuel Maverick for $20 a month.

Major Edwin B. Babbitt, the depot quartermaster, had recommended the Alamo be torn down and a warehouse be built to replace it. The quartermaster general, however, perhaps not out of a sense of history, but out of a sense that what was there could be saved, ordered the chapel repaired. So, Babbitt's forces erected a wooden roof over the main portion of the chapel, installed a second floor in the nave and repaired the façade. Part of the new façade was the parapet which gave the Alamo its world-famous silhouette. The repair bill came to $5,800, perhaps the best $5,800 ever spent to cement the historical legacy of Bexar County.

At the same time, the Army was renting the Vance Building, at Houston and St. Mary's Streets, and it served as the headquarters for the Department of Texas from 1848 to 1852 and 1855 to 1861. The break was due to the department being moved to Corpus Christi from 1852 to 1855, as the commander's physician had recommended he relocate to the coast to help his health.

Purchased in 1859, the only federally owned facility in Bexar before the Civil War was the San Antonio Arsenal, on sixteen acres between South Flores and the river. The facility, which was to replace the Alamo as a depot, was under construction when the war came and it was reoccupied after the war and completed in 1866. Today, the buildings on the property are excellent examples of adaptive reuse. They serve as the headquarters for the largest grocery chain in the area, H-E-B. The supermarket chain started in Kerrville in 1905 and opened its first Bexar County store in 1942, on Main Avenue north of downtown, on property now owned by VIA Metropolitan Transit. H-E-B observes its centennial in 2005. It has 41 stores in Bexar County, employing approximately 16,000 "partners." The firm has more than 300 stores in Texas and Mexico and employs more than 55,000 people.

The Post at San Antonio was a supply post for a large area of Texas, and transport of items was not always easy. Secretary of War Jefferson Davis approved what he thought was the perfect solution: Camels would be imported for transport. He convinced Congress it was a good plan. On June 4, 1856, Bexar County became the temporary camp site to thirty-four Army camels, quartered at San Pedro Springs. Later they were moved to Camp Verde, between Bandera and Kerrville. The camel experiment was somewhat successful, but the soldiers were not used to handling such often-difficult animals, and the smell of the animals was overwhelming. The remnants of the camel corps remained in military hands throughout the Civil War and up until 1866, when the last remaining forty-four camels were sold to Colonel Bethel Coopwood of San Antonio. Most of the animals were sold to private freight companies or wound up in circuses.

Opposite: Spanish presidial cavalry soldier equipped in accordance with the Royal Regulations of 1772 for presidios on the frontier. The key: 1. Jacket. 2. Riding whip. 3. Carbine. 4. Pouches for food and water. 5. Lance. 6. Pistols. 7. Shields. 8. Boots wih spurs. 9. Wood stirrups. 10. Carbine Box.
COURTESY OF THE FORT SAM HOUSTON MUSEUM.

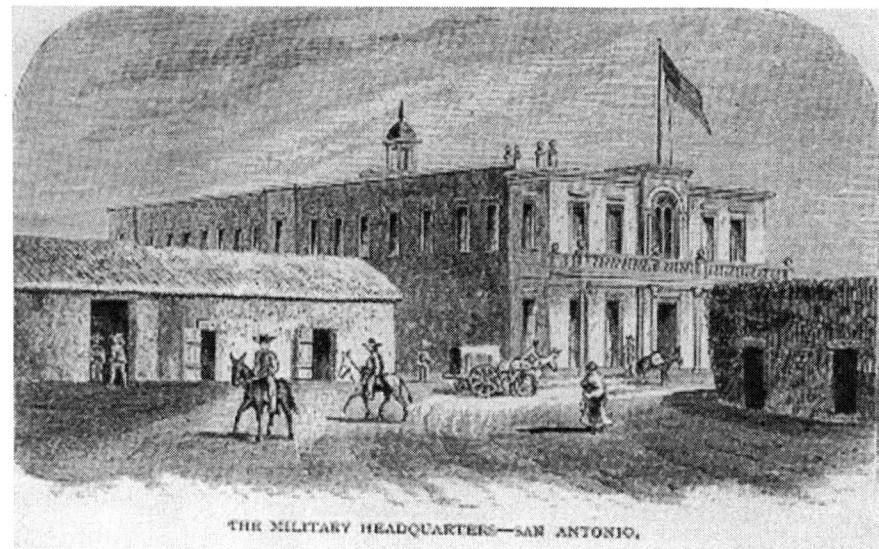

Above: The Military Headquarters in San Antonio in 1874.
COURTESY OF THE FORT SAM HOUSTON MUSEUM.

Top, right: Major Edwin Babbitt, who put the parapet on the Alamo.
COURTESY OF THE FORT SAM HOUSTON MUSEUM.

Below: The Arsenal in San Antonio in the 1870s.
COURTESY OF THE FORT SAM HOUSTON MUSEUM.

Much of the effort by the Army in Texas from the end of the Mexican War until the outbreak of the Civil War involved controlling the hostile Native American population. Between 1848 and 1861, Army troops in the state fought in 84 engagements against the Native Americans, accounting for 42 percent of all such engagements in that period.

By the end of 1860, it was apparent that the Southern states would secede from the Union. On February 16, 1861, secessionist forces seized military installations in Bexar and Brig. General David E. Twiggs surrendered all military personnel and materials at Plaza de las Islas on February 18. Bexar County, with its large German population, had been a center of anti-secession sentiment. Nevertheless, the county residents voted 827 to 709 for secession. Texas seceded from the Union on February 23, not quite two months before the Civil War began with the bombardment of Fort Sumter.

The only Civil War engagement in the area around Bexar County was the Battle of Adams Hill. It occurred on May 9, 1861, as federal forces under Lieutenant Colonel Isaac Van Duzer Reeve were evacuating Texas toward the coast. Confederates under Colonel Earl Van Dorn met up with the Union forces about fifteen miles west of downtown San Antonio on the military road to El Paso. The federal forces surrendered without a shot being fired.

During the war, some of the federal troops that had not fled to Union-held lands were held at a camp on Salado Creek in Bexar, while others were held at a camp near San Pedro Springs.

A letter from Fort Duncan, Texas, and letterhead, from 1869, showing well-known Bexar County scenes, including the missions and the use of camels by the military in the area. The letter is on Pentenrieder & Blersch pictorial letter paper.

COURTESY OF THE DAUGHTERS OF THE REPUBLIC OF TEXAS AT THE ALAMO DOCUMENTS COLLECTION AND THE INSTITUTE OF TEXAN CULTURES AT THE UNIVERSITY OF TEXAS AT SAN ANTONIO.

Chapter IV ♦ 47

Right: Lieutenant Colonel Robert E. Lee, as he served in Bexar County in the late 1860s.

COURTESY OF THE FORT SAM HOUSTON MUSEUM.

Below: General David Twiggs surrenders his Union Army command in San Antonio to Texan troops planning to join the Confederacy, February 16, 1861, in Plaza de las Islas. From Harper's Weekly, *March 23, 1861.*

COURTESY OF THE INSTITUTE OF TEXAN CULTURES AT THE UNIVERSITY OF TEXAS AT SAN ANTONIO.

Even though Bexar did not experience the devastation heaped on some other Southern areas during the war, the economy suffered drastically in the lack of markets and the uncertainty of Confederate currency. Also, there was a rash of vigilante activity, cattle rustling and Native American uprisings. After the war, U.S. troops returned to Bexar in September 1865, but the Post at San Antonio was not re-established until December 1866. For another decade, the Army leased space in the French Building, which had been the Confederate headquarters and was a building also used by the county, and in the Maverick Building on Houston Street.

The aftermath of the war had serious effects on the community. Land prices had been halved, farmlands were idle and taxes were scarce. Public sanitation suffered and there was a cholera outbreak in the 1860s. Floods caused serious damage to government property along the river, and both cholera and malaria struck the military. Also, the closest railroad connection was about sixty miles east, making movement of supplies difficult.

The military began talk of moving out of the county, which would have caused even a greater economic disaster. Rental of properties in San Antonio was costing the Army more than the operation of its headquarters in Philadelphia.

So, local governmental leaders began discussions to make land offers. After a long series of stops and starts, all settled on city-donated land and promise of a rail connection northeast of the city's downtown in a section which became known as Government Hill. Construction began in June 1876 on a quartermaster depot which came to be called the "Quadrangle." It was completed in 1878. During the next two years, the Army completed construction of a hospital and housing quarters.

As the railroad arrived and it became apparent that the physical location of Bexar County was key to military development, the Post at San Antonio grew rapidly. By 1890 it was the second largest military post in the nation, and the Army named it Fort Sam Houston. It has been the duty station of many famous Americans, including Dwight Eisenhower and Douglas MacArthur. One of the most famous people associated with the Quadrangle was the Apache Chief Geronimo, who was held captive there for a short time in 1886. During this period, thousands came to see the famous chief. Many myths have grown up around his stay there. One relates was that while he was held prisoner in the Quadrangle's tower, he jumped down, said to be the origin of the cry of "Geromino" while bailing out of an aircraft. Geronimo's jump did not occur.

Today, Fort Sam Houston remains a key component in the military mission of the nation. It housed the headquarters of the Fourth United States Army and now the Fifth United States Army and has been the home of major medical commands. It also hosts Brooke Army Medical Center (BAMC) and its world-famous burn treatment center in a new and larger facility in just the past few years. The original BAMC main building has been renovated and serves as the

Above: Troops in the Plaza de las Islas, February 1861, at the time of the surrender of the Union Army.
COURTESY OF THE FORT SAM HOUSTON MUSEUM.

Below: An early photo of construction of the Quadrangle at Fort Sam Houston, August 1876.
COURTESY OF THE FORT SAM HOUSTON MUSEUM.

headquarters of Army South. Fort Sam Houston has two museums, one medical and one military, and there are efforts by a hard-working preservation group to save many of the historical buildings on post.

Fort Sam Houston also was the site of one of the most controversial military developments in U.S. history—the Camp Logan riot, the first riot in the history of the nation in which more whites than African Americans lost their lives. The riot occurred in August 1917, after members of the all African-American Twenty-fourth Infantry Battalion stationed at Camp Logan outside Houston engaged a group in downtown Houston. The soldiers had been the victims of racial mistreatment, including an assault on some African-American soldiers by a white police officer. Twenty whites and four African Americans died in the riot. Courts martial of 118 soldiers were held in Gift Chapel at Fort Sam Houston in the largest murder trial in U. S. history. Thirteen African-American soldiers were found guilty and hanged on the banks of Salado Creek on the post with little public knowledge. Later, another six lost their lives by hanging.

On March 2, 1910, Bexar County began witnessing military aviation history. Lieutenant Benjamin Foulois, who had learned to fly through a correspondence course, climbed into the seat of his $150 Wright Brothers airplane at Fort Sam Houston. It was shipped in 17 crates and been assembled for $300. His flight at Arthur MacArthur Field at Fort Sam Houston lasted seven minutes. Although he reached only one hundred feet off the ground before he crashed, his feat was the first U.S. flight of a military-owned aircraft. By 1915, all six planes of the U.S. military were based at Fort Sam Houston. That same year, the Stinson family opened a flying school and airfield in south Bexar County. Today, Stinson Municipal Airport is the second oldest continuously operating civil airport in the nation.

Foulois' flight launched military aviation, which began to come into its own on April 5, 1917, at Kelly Field. This installation in southwest Bexar County was initially called San Antonio Flying Field and purchased by the military and renamed for George Edward Maurice Kelly. On May 11, 1911, at Fort Sam Houston, he became the first American military

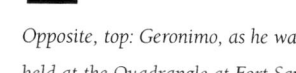

Opposite, top: Geronimo, as he was held at the Quadrangle at Fort Sam Houston in 1886.
COURTESY OF THE FORT SAM HOUSTON MUSEUM.

Opposite, bottom: The Fort Sam Houston courts-martial of African-American soldiers who had been serving at Camp Logan near Houston in a riot in 1917 was the largest murder trial ever held in the United States.
COURTESY OF MIKE KALISKI.

Left: This is the unmarked Fort Sam Houston Salado Creek burial ground of African-American soldiers hanged as a result of the Camp Logan riot.
COURTESY OF MIKE KALISKI.

Bottom, left: Lieutenant Benjamin D. Foulois, who made the first U.S. military flight in history.
COURTESY OF THE FORT SAM HOUSTON MUSEUM.

Bottom, right: Captain William M. Randolph, for whom Randolph Air Force Base in Bexar County was named.
COURTESY OF THE SAN ANTONIO EXPRESS-NEWS AND THE INSTITUTE OF TEXAN CULTURES AT THE UNIVERSITY OF TEXAS AT SAN ANTONIO.

aviator to die in the crash of a military airplane. When an aircraft landed at Kelly six years later, Kelly began its fame as the oldest, continuously active military airfield in the United States. Within months, the new airfield was providing training for hundreds of flying cadets, causing the military to open another air base, Brooks, nearby in Southern Bexar County. For five years all Army pilots received their wings in San Antonio, going through primary training at Brooks and advanced training at Kelly. One of the flying fields was Camp Kelly, established in 1916 and designated Kelly Field No. 1 in 1917. In 1926 it became Duncan Field, named for

Above: Lieutenant F. I. Patrick is shown with a 1924 aircraft in Bexar County.
COURTESY OF THE SAN ANTONIO EXPRESS-NEWS AND THE INSTITUTE OF TEXAN CULTURES AT THE UNIVERSITY OF TEXAS AT SAN ANTONIO.

Below: A scene during the filming of Wings *at Camp Stanley in Bexar County on September 19, 1926. The film won the first Academy Award as best picture.*
COURTESY OF THE INSTITUTE OF TEXAN CULTURES AT THE UNIVERSITY OF TEXAS AT SAN ANTONIO.

aviator Lieutenant Colonel Thomas Duncan, who was killed in a crash in 1923. It housed the Air Corps Training Center. In 1943 it merged with Kelly Field. Brooks closed after the end of World War I, but reopened in 1922. In 1926, legislation was passed for a third military aviation facility in Bexar County. Randolph Field was dedicated on June 20, 1930, as the world's largest air field and training center, and took over primary military air training.

There had been other developments, also. A balloon field, the first for the military, had opened in the Olmos Basin in 1917; *Wings*, the first movie to receive an Acadamy Award as best picture, had been filmed in Bexar County in 1926-27; air mail service was inaugurated in 1929; and the first combat parachute demonstrations took place at Brooks, also in 1929.

During World War II, the names of Kelly, Brooks, and Randolph, which eventually took on designations as Air Force bases, became part of the movie jargon, with such actors as John Wayne, Van Johnson, and Robert Taylor, who often noted that they had trained at one of these facilities. In 1942, the San Antonio Aviation Cadet Center, later to be named Lackland Air Force Base, was established, later to become the largest training base in the world. It remains the Air Force's basic training facility and Lackland's Wilford Hall Hospital is one of the most advanced in the area.

Above: A Wright Model "B" plane rests in a hangar at Stinson Field in Bexar County in 1918. The field is the second oldest civilian air base in the nation.
COURTESY OF THE SAN ANTONIO EXPRESS-NEWS AND THE INSTITUTE OF TEXAN CULTURES AT THE UNIVERSITY OF TEXAS AT SAN ANTONIO.

Left: An early flight line at Brooks Air Force Base in Bexar County.
COURTESY OF THE SAN ANTONIO EXPRESS-NEWS AND THE INSTITUTE OF TEXAN CULTURES AT THE UNIVERSITY OF TEXAS AT SAN ANTONIO.

Below: General Douglas MacArthur is hosted at the Alamo in 1951 by San Antonio Mayor Jack White.
COURTESY OF JOHN AND DELA WHITE AND THE INSTITUTE OF TEXAN CULTURES AT THE UNIVERSITY OF TEXAS AT SAN ANTONIO.

Above: The "Taj Mahal" is the headquarters building at Randolph Air Force Base.

Right: The old Brooke Army Medical Center at Fort Sam Houston was readied as the new home of Army South.

Below: The new Brooke Army Medical Center at Fort Sam Houston.

Kelly, Brooks, and Randolph took on varying kinds of missions in the decades after the war. Kelly became an air logistics center with its large civil service component maintaining major aircraft. Brooks became an important partner in aerospace development, focusing on man rather than machine. Randolph hosted the headquarters of the Air Education and Training Command, The Air Force Personnel Center, instructor pilot training, and joint navigation training with the U.S. Navy. The base's most-noted structure is its headquarters structure, the "Taj Mahal," which was built around a water tower. Kelly ceased its major military mission in 2001, becoming Kelly USA, a two-thousand-acre, master-planned business park with centers for aviation, office, logistical, and industrial needs in ten million square feet of space and with a two-mile runway. The Greater Kelly Development Authority, chartered to redevelop Kelly, has attracted major airline maintenance entities. Brooks now is Brooks City-Base, with properties taken over by the city and leased to the Air Force to effect cost savings. A business and technology park enhances economic development in the area.

EDUCATION

Growth of educational institutions ran parallel to other growth in the county. Among the earliest mention of a school in Bexar County is that in

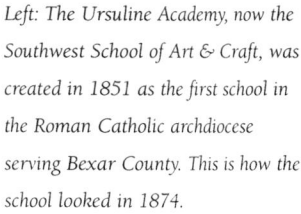

Left: The Ursuline Academy, now the Southwest School of Art & Craft, was created in 1851 as the first school in the Roman Catholic archdiocese serving Bexar County. This is how the school looked in 1874.

COURTESY OF CHARLES TOUDOUZE AND THE *SAN ANTONIO LIGHT* COLLECTION, THE INSTITUTE OF TEXAN CULTURES AT THE UNIVERSITY OF TEXAS AT SAN ANTONIO.

Below: This is how the German-English School, now part of a convocation center for a downtown hotel, looked in 1895.

COURTESY OF THE *SAN ANTONIO LIGHT* COLLECTION, THE INSTITUTE OF TEXAN CULTURES AT THE UNIVERSITY OF TEXAS AT SAN ANTONIO.

1789, José de la Mata asked the *cabildo*, the town council, to give official sanction to his private school. Also, the Spanish civil and military archives for Bexar County reveal that a school was maintained intermittently in Bexar with a schoolmaster paid out of the *mesteñas* fund, a tax collected on unbranded livestock, beginning in the 1770s. In the late 1820s, McClure's School served the children of new Anglo Americans coming into the area, but it was not until mid-century that education began to make a major mark.

The city created a free primary school system on February 1, 1853, and provided classes up to the eighth grade for children up to eighteen years of age. In 1871 the state took over the centralized school system, with the city regaining control in 1875 and opening a school within each of its four wards. The first school for African-American children opened in 1869. The high school opened in 1879, the fifth public high school in Texas and the only high school southwest of Kansas City to be included in the National Education Association Committee of Ten study on secondary education.

Four Ursuline nuns, three of whom were originally from France, arrived in San Antonio in 1851 from Galveston to establish the area's first private school for girls on the banks of the San Antonio River. The next year two Irish Ursuline nuns followed. They described their trip this way: "The roads are nothing more than pathways beaten through the prairies. You can scarcely imagine anything so horrible as the Texian mud. The bogs of old Ireland could never come up to this." Yet, the Sisters created the first Catholic school in San Antonio and the second recognized formal school for girls in the state. For more than 140 years, the school educated young ladies of the city. It moved from its original location on the river to an outlying area in 1965 and eventually closed in 1992. Its outlying campus now is the location of a Christian school. The downtown campus was purchased by the San Antonio Conservation Society, rebuilt and converted into the Southwest School of Art & Craft. Today, it not only is an important arts center, but its gardens are the scene of some of the most memorable social affairs in the city.

Today's Catholic Archdiocese of San Antonio covers 19 counties, but most of its schools are in Bexar County—7 of the 8 high schools, 31 of the 39 middle/junior high schools and 31 of the 39 elementary schools. The Bexar Catholic school enrollment is 13,699 students. Most students attend school in Bexar County's thirteen public school districts, most of them wholly within the county. A few districts spill over to adjacent counties, and several school districts from bordering counties spill over into Bexar. There also are three military school districts within the county that are associated with Randolph AFB, Lackland AFB, and Fort Sam Houston.

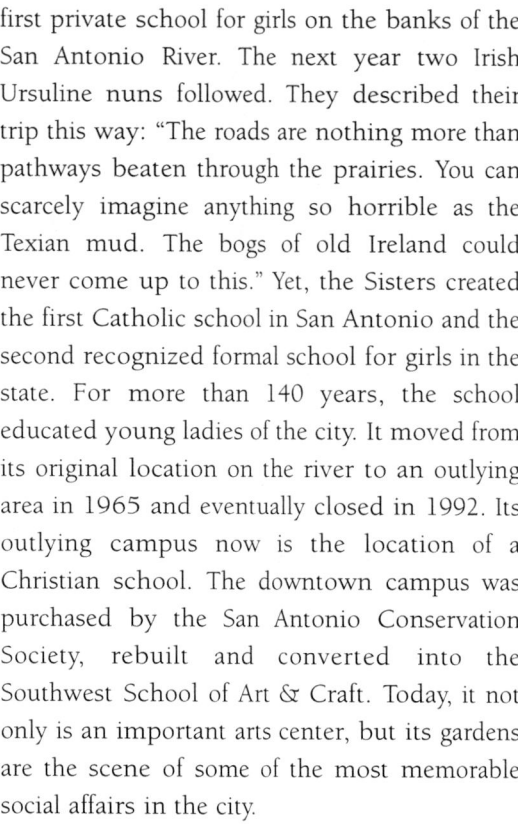

There are hundreds of elementary and junior/middle schools in the 16 districts, and more than 40 high schools. The rapidly growing county dictates continuing school construction. Enrollment in the districts runs from over 60,000 in the Northside School District to little more than 1,000 students in the individual military districts. The Northside District is one of the largest in the state, both by student count and geographic size, 355 square miles. One of the smaller districts in the county, by enrollment, East Central, has a land area of 360 square miles.

Most of the districts in the county were created in the 1940s, 1950s, and 1960s with the consolidation of rural school districts, but some have histories even older. One district, Harlandale, traces its history to 1888, when classes were held in the granary of San José Mission. One of the middle schools in that district is at the site of a former famous swimming pool and spa, Terrell Wells, which drew famous people from around the world as customers. And, the East Central District was the consolidation of 24 rural districts which included schools formed by German, Polish and Czech immigrants from the middle 1800s. The East Central administrative complex includes the historic two-room rural Boidtvelde School,

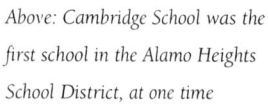

Above: Cambridge School was the first school in the Alamo Heights School District, at one time serving eleven grades.
COURTESY OF ALAMO HEIGHTS SCHOOL DISTRICT.

Below: Bluebonnet School served the children of the employees of Cementville, the cement plant area that now is a shopping mall.
COURTESY OF ALAMO HEIGHTS SCHOOL DISTRICT.

restored and listed on the National Register of Historical Places.

The San Antonio public schools became independent of city control in 1899 and the first board of education elected. George W. Brackenridge was the first president. The new independent school district was chartered in 1903. In 1923 a comprehensive junior school system was implemented as the first in Texas, perhaps the nation. Two years later, the district opened San Antonio Junior College. In 1930, Thomas Jefferson High School opened and was named by Life Magazine as the "most beautiful" in the United States. In 1940 the district opened its major sports facility, Alamo Stadium, at the south end of the Olmos Basin, and in 1945, opened Eloise Japhet School, the first school in Texas for handicapped students.

Even though three smaller school districts, Los Angeles Heights, Hot Wells (the site of a world-famous spa), and W. W. White, joined the San Antonio District in the 1940s, the district had been prohibited by court edict from expanding as the city annexed new areas. Despite the prohibition for territorial growth, student enrollment in the district peaked at more

Above: Jefferson High School in the San Antonio School District, when it was built in 1930 was called by Life Magazine *"the most beautiful school in America."*
COURTESY OF FLORENCE COLLETTE AYRES AND THE INSTITUTE OF TEXAN CULTURES AT THE UNIVERSITY OF TEXAS AT SAN ANTONIO.

Below: The Hot Wells Sanitarium, designed by Alfred Giles.
COURTESY OF F. A. SCHMIDT AND THE INSTITUTE OF TEXAN CULTURES AT THE UNIVERSITY OF TEXAS AT SAN ANTONIO.

than seventy-six thousand about 1970. The population erosion of the inner city then began to slice pupil enrollment.

Alamo Heights Independent School District, partly in the suburban city of Alamo Heights and partly in San Antonio, began in 1909, and is listed as the county's top "property rich" district. The North East and Northside Districts are not far behind. In Texas, there long has been a controversy in financing public elementary and secondary education, as income is based both on a state formula of reimbursement and on local property taxes. The variation in tax base among school districts has raised the question of equal education for all Texas students. Because of this, some have called on the state to demand the richer districts share their wealth. The "Robin Hood" state school finance plan came about in large part because of advocates for Edgewood Independent School District, a small and poor school district in Bexar County. That district has a student body of predominately Hispanic students.

The Alamo Heights Independent School District started with a two-room wooden schoolhouse, Cambridge, which housed all of the students, at that time consisting of grades one through eleven. The district's current athletic field was constructed in 1938 as a WPA project, and is adjacent to the high school built later in 1949-50. The district had won its first district football championship in 1926, under the Coach Earl "Mule" Frazier. The Alamo Heights Mules take their name from this coach, not from a stubborn animal. The Heights district, ironically, long included one of the poorest school areas in the county. Bluebonnet School, in a quarry area mini-town called Cementville, served the children of workers at a cement plant that eventually was closed. The plant site now is a large commercial mall development, the Quarry Market, at the northern edge of the Olmos Basin.

Judson School District in northeast Bexar County serves primarily the suburban cities of Converse, Kirby, and Selma, at the edge of Randolph Air Force Base. Judson High School

Above: William C. Rote was the second superintendent of the San Antonio School District and the man who divided the schools into grades and organized the county's first high school, in 1879.
COURTESY OF THE SAN ANTONIO SCHOOL DISTRICT.

Below: Judson High School in Converse in Bexar County is one of the largest schools in the state.
COURTESY OF THE JUDSON SCHOOL DISTRICT.

has split campuses for freshman/sophomores and juniors/seniors and is one of the five largest high schools in the state, with a student body of nearly forty-eight hundred students. After a sharply contested election, voters approved a second high school. The Judson district was named for Moses Judson, who drilled the first artesian well in Bexar County and who was superintendent of the San Antonio Water Works Company. It was the forerunner of the San Antonio Water System, the city's current chief water provider.

In terms of early and unified primary and secondary education in Bexar, the San Antonio District remains the leader. It covers 79 square miles in the center of the county within the City of San Antonio and has 8 high schools, 17 middle schools, 63 elementary schools, and 4 special campuses, with a total student enrollment of just beyond 56,500. Of special interest has been the creation of magnet schools offering specialties such as art and business. This district has created these schools within schools. Northside began the first, Health Careers High School, which stands as an independent magnet school. Northside also has a communications arts high school and North East, an international school. Many other magnet schools also operate within existing schools in the San Antonio ISD and elsewhere.

Bexar County also is the home of a large number of private schools, most of them church-related. One of these is Texas Military Institute, which was founded in 1893 on Government Hill near Fort Sam Houston by the Episcopal Church as the West Texas Military Academy. In that school's 1897 graduating class was a cadet who graduated in the top of his class at West Point in 1903. His name: Douglas MacArthur. The academy moved into Alamo Heights in 1910. In 1926, it merged with the upper school of San Antonio Academy and became TMI, under a private corporation. It returned to church affiliation in 1953 and became coed in 1972. In 1989, the school moved to the far northwest side of the county,

Above: Dwight Eisenhower, shown with his wife Mamie, was a coach at St. Mary's University in 1916.
COURTESY OF ST. MARY'S UNIVERSITY.

Below: The main building of the University of the Incarnate Word, founded by the Sisters of Charity of the Incarnate Word.

close to an exclusive subdivision, the Dominion. Among the school's graduates over its 110 years of operation have been 13 generals, a Medal of Honor recipient, five Distinguished Cross recipients, two bishops, an astronaut, an ambassador, a congressman, many bank and college presidents, a noted painter, Rhodes scholars, and television stars. Other prominent private schools include St. Mary's Hall, Providence High School, San Antonio Academy, and Keystone School.

Besides Bexar's large contingent of elementary- and secondary-level schools, the county is the home to significant institutions of higher learning. Four brothers of the Society of Mary, the Marianists, arrived in San Antonio by stagecoach in 1852 and founded the St. Mary's School for Boys. Classes began with twelve students in temporary quarters atop a livery stable on Military Plaza. The permanent school began shortly thereafter on land sold by John Twohig, just east of his house on the river. The school was chartered by the state in 1882 as St. Mary's College. The "Brothers' School" expanded into St. Mary's Institute. Later, due to lack of space, land was purchased in 1930 on North St. Mary's Street, along the river. The new school opened in January 1932 with a new name: Central Catholic High School. It is now the oldest and largest all boys' school in Texas. Graduates have included such prominent leaders as former Mayor Henry Cisneros.

St. Mary's College was overcrowded and the Marianists decided to find a separate place for the boarding department. The West End Town Company offered the Marianists a seventy-three-acre tract in Woodlawn Hills in the northwest section of the county for $1, with the provision that they build another college. It became part of the university in 1934, using space vacated by the high school. Classes at St. Louis College opened on the site on September 4, 1894. In 1923, the colleges were consolidated at the site as St. Mary's College, becoming St. Mary's University in 1926. The School of Law, founded in 1927, remained downtown, and became part of the university in 1934. In 1963, the university went coed. The downtown campus today is a major hotel, utilizing the historic St. Mary's structures in adaptive reuse.

In 2004, St. Mary's University had an enrollment of more than four thousand students in its three undergraduate schools, the graduate school and the law school. The school has taught many of the leading citizens of the

Above: The Motherhouse Chapel of the Sisters of Charity.

Right: The grounds of the Urrutia mansion, across the street from the University of the Incarnate Word.

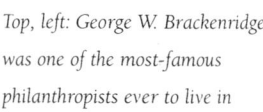

Top, left: George W. Brackenridge was one of the most-famous philanthropists ever to live in Bexar County.
COURTESY OF THE SAN ANTONIO LIGHT COLLECTION, THE INSTITUTE OF TEXAN CULTURES AT THE UNIVERSITY OF TEXAS AT SAN ANTONIO.

Top, right: This sculpture of George Brackenridge is found at the eastern entrance to Brackenridge Park.

Below: Our Lady of the Lake University was founded in 1895 by the Sisters of Divine Providence.
COURTESY OF OUR LADY OF THE LAKE UNIVERSITY.

community and won NCAA championships in baseball and softball and NAIA championships in softball and men's basketball. Dwight Eisenhower was a coach there around 1916.

Not far south and east of St. Mary's University, at the edge of Elmendorf Lake, is Our Lady of the Lake University. It was established as Our Lady of the Lake Academy in 1895 by the Sisters of Divine Providence, a religious order formed in the eighteenth century in Lorraine, France. The sisters had arrived in Texas in 1866 and formed a school in Castroville in 1867. The first college program offered at the San Antonio school began in 1911 as a two-year curriculum for women. In 1919 the program was expanded to four years and coed graduate study began in 1942. In 1923, OLLU became the first San Antonio institution of higher learning to receive regional accreditation. In 1969 the entire program became coed and the school became a university in 1975. A weekend degree program began in 1978, expanding to Houston in 1986 and Dallas in 1994. Today, OLLU has an enrollment of 3,300 students in 58 areas of study in bachelor's studies, 23 in master's, and two in doctoral. The 193-foot spire of the Gothic-design chapel at the school is a landmark in West Bexar County.

When completed in 1923 it was the tallest structure in Bexar County.

At the headwaters of the San Antonio River in north central Bexar County, at the edge of the Olmos Basin and the suburban City of Alamo Heights stands the University of the Incarnate Word, a school so wrapped up in the story of the area that it takes on extra significance to those who believe that history casts a special spell. In 1852 the City of San Antonio sold this property to Alderman (later Mayor) J. R. Sweet who built his home there. George Washington

Chapter IV ♦ 61

The Brackenridge Villa on the grounds of the University of the Incarnate Word once was Fernridge, the home of George Brackenridge, at the headwaters of the San Antonio River.

Brackenridge, whose family had moved to Texas from Indiana, was a brilliant and shrewd businessman who became one of the most important philanthropists in the history of Bexar County. He made a fortune in the depressed cotton market following the Civil War; founded the first national bank in San Antonio; gained control of the city's waterworks; invested in railroads, factories, and publishing companies; and acquired real estate which later became Fort Sam Houston, Brackenridge Park, the San Antonio Country Club, and the City of Alamo Heights. He purchased 108 acres from Sweet in 1869, in the name of his mother Isabel. He occupied the Sweet homestead with his mother and sister, Eleanor, and renamed the house Fernridge ("bracken" is the Scottish word for fern) and he named the entire estate Alamo Heights. He expanded Fernridge to a three-story Victorian structure. Late in the century, with the death of his mother, he offered to sell the property back to the city but a deal could not be struck.

Now enter the Sisters of Charity of the Incarnate Word, a French order which took its name from Biblical references to Jesus as the Incarnate Word, God having been given human form. While San Antonio suffered with cholera after the Civil War, Galveston Bishop Claude Dubuis recruited three sisters of the order to come to San Antonio to care for the sick in his diocese. The sisters, led by Mother Madeleine Chollet, founded an infirmary which became Santa Rosa Medical Center, as well as an orphanage and set out to purchase land to build a college. In 1896, Mother Madeleine found forty acres she liked, land that belonged to George Brackenridge at the headwaters of the river. Brackenridge, however, did not want to sell just 40 acres; he wanted to sell his entire estate, 280 acres, for $120,000. The sisters took out a twenty-five-year note, bought the property and renamed Fernridge "Brackenridge Villa." The shrewd Brackenridge was astounded

Above: The Sisters of Charity founded Santa Rosa Hospital.
COURTESY OF CHRISTUS SANTA ROSA HOSPITAL.

Left: Santa Rosa Hospital is viewed from Market Square and Milam Park, from an August 25, 1910, postcard.
COURTESY OF ROBERT ASHCROFT AND THE INSTITUTE OF TEXAN CULTURES AT THE UNIVERSITY OF TEXAS AT SAN ANTONIO.

Below: CHRISTUS Santa Rosa Hospital as it appears today.
COURTESY OF CHRISTUS SANTA ROSA HOSPITAL

Chapter IV ✦ 63

Right: Trinity University was built by the lift-slab method, in which complete floors were formed and lifted into place.
COURTESY OF TRINITY UNIVERSITY.

Below: Trinity University as it appears today.

when the sisters not only did not default the loan, but never missed a payment. Brackenridge Villa became the nuns' motherhouse. They then built a new motherhouse, chartered a college, opening it to students in 1910, added to their Santa Rosa Hospital (now CHRISTUS Santa Rosa) downtown and constructed a high school. They also formed other schools and hospitals across the nation.

As a university, the sisters' college now has an enrollment of nearly forty-three hundred students and has developed into a large expanse of attractive buildings. Its School of Nursing continues to carry on the early tradition of healing in the community, and its grounds include the Blue Hole, the spring which sends forth the waters forming the San Antonio River. The Brackenridge Villa, almost destroyed by fire in 1983, has been renovated and now not only serves as a community meeting place and university offices, but also as a reminder of the rich heritage of the Brackenridge family and the tenacity of a small group of nuns who arrived in Bexar County nearly 140 years ago.

Just across U.S. 281 and a bit south of the University of the Incarnate Word is Trinity University, built on a quarry bluff overlooking

the city. It is called the "Skyline Campus." Trinity was formed in 1869 in Tehuacana from three Presbyterian colleges that had closed. The unified school moved to Waxahachie and, in 1942, to west Bexar County. In 1950 the school moved and created a campus of innovative engineering design. The new Trinity used the lift-slab method of construction, in which floors were constructed and lifted into place. In 2003, the first building constructed on the campus with this method was torn down and a new hall put up in its place. Trinity had official ties to the Presbyterian Church until 1969 when they were dissolved in the school's hundredth year. Today, Trinity has an outstanding reputation as one of the finest small colleges in the nation, earned by the awards it wins constantly. It has an enrollment of twenty-four hundred students.

In 1969, San Antonio anchored the only urban region in the state not served by a public university. On June 5 of that year, the Texas Legislature founded the University of Texas at San Antonio as part of The University of Texas System. A major community discussion on whether the university would be located downtown, in the southern part of the county or in the northwest caused a division in civic forces for a time. Not until 1976 did the university have a permanent campus, when seven major buildings were completed on a six-hundred-acre tract in the foothills of northwest Bexar County. UTSA construction was the largest building project in higher education in the nation at the time.

UTSA has experienced unprecedented growth in its thirty-five-year history. It has a student body of more than twenty-two thousand students and added a downtown campus to complement its outlying properties. It offers ninety-three degree programs, recently established the Institute of Law and Public Affairs, and the new science complex is one of the largest in Texas.

Bexar County also has one of the most-expansive junior college programs in the nation,

Above: The main campus of the University of Texas at San Antonio is in far west Bexar County.
COURTESY OF THE UNIVERSITY OF TEXAS AT SAN ANTONIO.

Below: The University of Texas at San Antonio has a campus near the center of the city.
COURTESY OF THE UNIVERSITY OF TEXAS AT SAN ANTONIO.

Chapter IV ♦ 65

Above: St. Louis Hall on the campus of St. Mary's University.
COURTESY OF ST. MARY'S UNIVERSITY.

Below: This photo by Al Mogavero, taken before March 1, 1898, is of a session of the St. Philip's Saturday Evening Sewing Class, the predecessor to St. Philip's College.

addressing a large variety of interests in various areas of the county. The Alamo Community College District consists of four colleges with several branch campuses. St. Philip's College, formed in 1898, now has two campuses, one in the eastern part of the county, the other in the southwestern sector. San Antonio College is near downtown San Antonio. It was founded in 1925. Palo Alto College, in the southern part of the county, opened in 1985 and Northwest Vista College, on the west side of the county, in 1995. Combined they have a total enrollment of nearly 45,000 students, with another 18,000 students in continuing education classes. This comprises the second largest college district in Texas, with the 5,250 employees of the district making it the sixteenth largest employer in the area. The site for a fifth college for the district has been selected in the far northeast area of the county near the town of Live Oak.

In 1897 some of the parishioners of St. Philip's Church, which had been formed in 1895, felt that African-American students should be offered wider educational opportunities than those received in the public schools. Laura Jackson, a popular local seamstress, offered to teach a sewing class if church members would organize it. The church members opened the Saturday Evening Sewing Class in the church rectory. James Steptoe Johnston, Bishop of the Protestant Episcopal Church in the Missionary District of Western Texas, took note of the rapid growth of the class. He had witnessed the eagerness of freedmen to learn and he vowed to create a school that would enable African Americans to take a more productive role in society. On March 1, 1898, the St. Philip's Vocational School for Colored Children opened at the church in La Villita with Alice Cowan as the first headmistress.

In 1902, Artemisia Bowden, a teacher and daughter of a former slave, assumed leadership of the school. She led the school, over a period of fifty-two years, from a small parochial school to a two-year accredited college. In 1917 the school moved from the church to a new location just east of downtown San Antonio. In 1942, the school became affiliated with San Antonio College and the San Antonio School District and transitioned from a private to public enterprise.

In 1945, St. Philip's and San Antonio College formed the San Antonio Union Junior College District, now the Alamo Community College District. In 1987 the southwest campus of St. Philip's, which had been an extension site on the former East Kelly Air Force Base, became an official campus. St. Philip's rapid growth in recent years has included adding a literacy center for the City of San Antonio.

San Antonio College was established as University Junior College in September 1925, under the auspices of The University of Texas. The first classes were held at Main Avenue High School. The following year, control of the college went to the San Antonio School District, and the name was changed to San Antonio Junior College. It operated in the old German-English School building on South Alamo Street. In 1951 the college opened its present campus on San Pedro Avenue across from San Pedro Springs Park.

The opening of Palo Alto College in 1985 was a significant development in South Bexar County, historically an underserved section of the community. Hispanics comprise more than

Above: Dr. Artemisia Bowden was the person who built St. Philip's College.
COURTESY OF ST. PHILIP'S COLLEGE.

Below: Today, St. Philip's College is the home of one of the area's major literacy centers.

half the college's enrollment, and there are more female than male students. For the first two years, the college offices were located at Billy Mitchell Village near Kelly Air Force Base, and classes were held at various high schools and military installations. The current 111-acre campus was opened in 1987, and by 1991 Palo Alto was the fastest-growing community college in Texas.

Because of the rapid growth of Palo Alto and because it was drawing students from the western part of the county, as well as from nearby rural areas, Northwest Vista College opened. It is located on a 137-acre tract in the northwest section of the county, near Sea World, a major entertainment complex. The rapid growth of the community college population and demands on the four-year colleges in the county have prompted the formation of a branch campus of Texas A&M University-Kingsville (the home of the famous King Ranch in South Texas) to serve the southern sector of Bexar County.

WORSHIP

As educational developments were unfolding in Bexar County near the turn of the nineteenth century, religion was taking on new roles in the community. In the beginning, the Native American population had bowed to nature. In the 16th, 17th, and 18th centuries, the padres of the Roman Catholic Church came and there were few Protestants (none officially) in the area. Even today, officials of the San Antonio Community of Churches estimate that 300,000 of the people in the county profess to be Roman Catholics, with another 100,000 following practices of various forms of the Baptist Church, primarily Southern Baptist.

Above: Travis Park Methodist Church was one of the early Protestant churches in Bexar County.

Below: Robert E. Lee was one of the founders of St. Mark's Episcopal Church in San Antonio.

In 1844 a Presbyterian missionary, John McCullough, and a Methodist missionary, John Wesley DeVilbiss, both circuit riders, conducted the first Protestant services in the county. The site of the service was near today's West Commerce and Soledad Streets. The following year, McCullough accepted an invitation of the Presbyterian Board of Foreign Missions to establish a church in San Antonio. In 1846 he organized a congregation that was to become First Presbyterian Church, and he formed a day school for Mexican children. That school became the basis for the formation of the free school system in the city, taken on by the school district. Life was difficult for men of the cloth in Bexar. After there was an attempt on his life in 1849, McCullough left, never to return. The church he founded, originally a small adobe building, on McCullough Avenue, today is one of the leading churches of downtown San Antonio.

The Methodists formed their own church in 1852, and it became Travis Park Methodist Church. The Episcopalians founded St. Mark's Church in 1850. One of the organizers of this church was an Army officer named Robert E. Lee, who later resigned his commission to accept the leadership of the military forces of the Confederate States of America. St. Mark's also is on Travis Park, cater-cornered from Travis Park Methodist, and the two churches join First Presbyterian as some of the leading churches in the city today. Travis Park had been Samuel Maverick's orchard and he gave it to the city. The Baptists organized a church in 1851 and the Evangelical Lutheran Church was organized in the city in 1857.

Bexar County has many beautiful and inviting churches, including the renovated San Fernando Cathedral, the chapels at Our Lady of the Lake University and the University of the Incarnate Word and the Marguerite B. Parker Chapel at Trinity University. The small mission churches and the Basilica of the National Shrine of the Little Flower also deserve a mention, as do the Protestant churches already discussed and those serving many other Roman Catholic, Protestant, and charismatic doctrines, synagogues and churches serving Greek and Maronite communities.

One of the most unusual of the churches is St. Joseph's Downtown Church, built in 1868 to serve German Catholic immigrants. The stations of the cross in that church are in both English and German. In 1945 the department store next door to the church, Joske's of Texas, then the largest store in the state, offered to purchase the church property so the store could be expanded. When the parishioners turned down the offer, the department store built the store's addition

St. Joseph's Catholic Church in the center city served the German population. This image is copied from an original stereograph by Alexis V. Latourette, c. 1877.

COURTESY OF THE SAN ANTONIO CONSERVATION SOCIETY AND THE INSTITUTE OF TEXAN CULTURES AT THE UNIVERSITY OF TEXAS AT SAN ANTONIO.

The Mt. Zion Baptist Church, shown here in a photograph taken at a previous location of the church in the early 1900s, long has served East Bexar County.
COURTESY OF THE REVEREND CLAUDE BLACK AND THE INSTITUTE OF TEXAN CULTURES AT THE UNIVERSITY OF TEXAS AT SAN ANTONIO.

around the church, and the church became a jewel encircled by the store, now called Dillard's and part of the Rivercenter Mall.

Another church of note is the Little Church of La Villita, a nondenominational church in the La Villita complex on the river. The church was formed in 1871 by the Reverend Gustav Elley, an ancestor to former Bexar County State Senator Glenn Kothmann, as the German Methodist Episcopal Church. It moved to the south side of the city as Hackberry Street Methodist Church in 1895, when the city took over the La Villita site.

The Jewish population in Bexar remains small, but quite active in civic affairs. Dr. Albert Levy was a surgeon for the *Texian* revolutionaries and was involved with forces that gained control of San Antonio in 1835, the action that touched off Santa Anna's march into South Texas. The first synagogue, Temple Beth-El, was formed in San Antonio in the 1870s as the oldest synagogue in South Texas. It was predated by a Jewish cemetery just east of downtown San Antonio, a cemetery which still exists. Today the city has active Reformed, Conservative, and Orthodox synagogues and there is a colorful Israeli festival. The Jewish contribution to Bexar County far outreaches the percentage of those of that faith in the county.

Bexar County has been an area to serve diverse religious beliefs. For instance, the county has four Buddhist temples, the first which was formed in the 1980s on the farm of the Barrows family by the Lao/Thai community. The Buddhist influence also has a major tie to the Vietnamese population, and there are also local Buddhists of many backgrounds, including Chinese. Many members of "mainline" congregations also take advantage of meditation sessions provided by local Buddhist organizations. There has been a recent proliferation of Korean churches, with seven churches in the county tied to various denominations, including Methodist, Baptist, Presbyterian and gospel churches. The oldest of these, the Korean Presbyterian Church, was thirty years old the summer of 2004. The Korean churches provide services both in Korean and in English.

The county also has Islamic organizations that serve a diverse population. Dr. Najah M. Al-Shalchi believes the first Muslim residents of San Antonio were either students seeking an education in local institutions or African Americans who had been converted to Islam. One of the earliest mosques in the area was on the grounds of Lackland Air Force Base in the late 1960s. One of the oldest mosques of San Antonio is Luqman's Masjid, on Hays Street, on the northeast side of downtown. It serves primarily the African-American Muslim community. In the mid-1980s a part-time Islamic Sunday school, Al-Madina, was established in a home in Helotes. In 1991 the Islamic Center was established, and a mosque eventually was built on Fairhaven, in the northwest area of San Antonio. This was the largest mosque in the history of the city. Amana Academy began operation as a full-time school. In 2004 the school had about thirty students enrolled and the school offered a regular school curriculum, as well as Arabic and Islamic studies. Al-Shalchi points out that the diversity of the Muslim community in Bexar County includes members from the Middle East, India, Pakistan, Iran, Southeast Asia, Sub-Saharan Africa, North Africa, and Europe, as well as American-born Muslims. Members of the Muslim community are involved in professions such as teaching, law, medicine, accounting, and private entrepreneurship, and college students continue to make up a significant portion of the community.

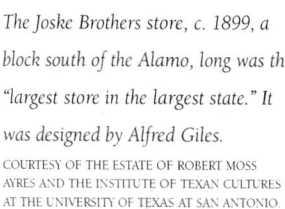

The Joske Brothers store, c. 1899, a block south of the Alamo, long was the "largest store in the largest state." It was designed by Alfred Giles.

COURTESY OF THE ESTATE OF ROBERT MOSS AYRES AND THE INSTITUTE OF TEXAN CULTURES AT THE UNIVERSITY OF TEXAS AT SAN ANTONIO.

CHAPTER V

THE GOLDEN AGE IN BEXAR

At the end of the nineteenth century, the character of life in Bexar County had begun to change. The U.S. Census of 1890 indicated that more of the county's inhabitants had been born in Germany (4,039) than had been born in Mexico (3,561). Even though the railroad had caused many smaller communities to spring up in the county, 37,673 of the county's 49,266 still lived within the limits of San Antonio. The manufacturing sector was growing, and the agricultural economy was picking up rapidly. Between 1880 and 1920 the number of farms more than doubled, up to more than 3,200, with 800,000 acres under cultivation. However, operators owned fewer than half of the farms, and tenant workers were paid low wages. Even though Bexar County never was considered oil country, there was a steady rise in oil production from its first discovery in the area in December 1887, when George Dulling struck oil while drilling an artesian well near current-day Brooks City-Base. Oil production continued until the early 1990s, when the output was more than 32.5 million barrels. On the downtown plazas the county's famous chili queens operated what were the first outdoor restaurants in the area. Their operations had sprung up because chili con carne was a Bexar County invention, sometime in the 1840s. The chili queens continued in operation until the late 1930s, when health concerns shut them down. In the southern area of the county, off Presa Street, the Hot Wells hotel and spa had begun operation, promoting its well-known sulphur waters to the rich and famous from around the world. The wells still flow, but the spa ceased operation in the early 1920s. The restaurant at Hot Wells was still in operation in the 1960s, until destroyed by fire.

On November 12, 1888, the residents of Bexar County began an adventure which lasted for twenty-three years. With an investment of $25,749.02, an eighty-acre international exposition opened in what is now Riverside Park, on the south side. Mexican President Porfirio Díaz pushed a telegraph key in Mexico City to open the San Antonio International Exposition, which brought products and many visitors from Mexico. The fair included the showing of prize livestock, horse racing, and later, auto racing, the playing of the first football game between the Texas Longhorns and the Texas Aggies, and the training of Teddy Roosevelt's Rough Riders. In his Retama race track offices in north Bexar County, Joe Straus Jr., a leading San Antonio businessman, proudly exhibits photos of his grandfather and other leading area businessmen promoting the exposition. A line for electric streetcars connected the center of the city to the fair grounds. This international fair ended its run after the Mexican Revolution burst onto the scene in 1910. It was often called the first HemisFair which opened in San Antonio in 1968.

Many interesting things occurred in Bexar besides the fair. Francisco Madero planned the 1910 revolution in his room at the Hutchins Hotel, in several private residences and in Milam Park, near CHRISTUS Santa Rosa Medical Center. The plans were printed in San Antonio. The hospital, built by the Sisters of Charity of the Incarnate Word, is also near Market Square, a modern-day version of the *mercado* which operated there in earlier days. The old Market House had been designed by architect Alfred Giles near the turn of the century, to include refrigeration and running water. The structure was razed in the late 1930s to make way for more modern structures.

The area's first traffic signal light was installed opposite the I&GN Depot on Commerce Street in 1890. The next year, the county's first professional fire company, owning two horse-drawn steam pumpers, went into operation. That same year there were four street car companies operating, but in 1901 they were consolidated into one, the San Antonio Traction Company. By 1905, vehicular traffic included conveyances powered by horse, electricity, gasoline and steam. Seven years later an ordinance required all automobiles to be numbered.

Opposite: The melding of the old and the new is shown dramatically in this photo of Haymarket Plaza west of the downtown area, as vegetable trucks and covered wagons meet, c. 1925. Most of the area was torn down to make way for a freeway.
COURTESY OF SAN ANTONIO EXPRESS-NEWS AND THE INSTITUTE OF TEXAN CULTURES AT THE UNIVERSITY OF TEXAS AT SAN ANTONIO.

Above: A photograph by N. M. Wilcox of downtown San Antonio and the Alamo in the 1920s.
COURTESY OF THE ARCHIVES DIVISION OF THE TEXAS STATE LIBRARY.

Below: Chili stands on downtown plazas were the county's first outdoor restaurants. This one operated on Military Plaza in the 1880s.
COURTESY OF THE ESTATE OF ROBERT MOSS AYRES AND THE INSTITUTE OF TEXAN CULTURES AT THE UNIVERSITY OF TEXAS AT SAN ANTONIO.

Mass transportation also developed. In 1902 the Southern Pacific opened a depot on East Commerce Street. In 1906 the I&GN, which became the Missouri Pacific, began construction of a depot on the city's near West Side, at Commerce and Medina. That building, with a sculpture of a Native American on top, now is the headquarters for a credit union. In 1917 the Missouri-Kansas-Texas Depot began operation at Durango and South Flores, but that depot no longer exists. Also in 1917 the San Antonio Traction Company and the San Antonio Gas & Electric Company consolidated into the San Antonio Public Service Company. The new company built the area's first motorized bus to serve Fort Sam Houston.

Many developments occurred in government also over the same period. During the time of the Republic of Texas, the county board had been composed of a chief justice and justices of the peace. Under constitutions in 1845, 1861, and 1866, four elected commissioners had replaced the JPs, but the Constitution of 1869 had put JPs back in as directors. The Texas Constitution of 1876 had established a new form of county government, creating for each county a Commissioners Court composed of a county judge, as presiding officer, and four commissioners, each elected from a precinct.

Under the Constitution of 1876, still in force and much-amended, the county court actually was not a court in the usual sense, but a general

Top: Noted architect Atlee B. Ayres shows off his one-cylinder Ford in 1904. The vehicle, the eighth auto in the city, was purchased second hand by Ayres from R. N. Hughes, a neighbor, for $250.
<small>COURTESY OF ANN RUSSELL AND THE INSTITUTE OF TEXAN CULTURES AT THE UNIVERSITY OF TEXAS AT SAN ANTONIO.</small>

Middle: Atlee B. Ayres and his sons Robert and Atlee T. are in the third car from the left in this Sunday morning auto meet, in 1906.
<small>COURTESY OF ANN RUSSELL AND THE INSTITUTE OF TEXAN CULTURES AT THE UNIVERSITY OF TEXAS AT SAN ANTONIO.</small>

Bottom: Bexar County hosted an international fair for twenty-three years on Mission Road and the San Antonio River. The International Fair and Exposition closed because of the Mexican Revolution of 1910.
<small>COURTESY OF SAN ANTONIO EXPRESS-NEWS AND THE INSTITUTE OF TEXAN CULTURES AT THE UNIVERSITY OF TEXAS AT SAN ANTONIO.</small>

Right: The Market House east of the Bexar County Courthouse was closed to make way for river and street improvements.
COURTESY OF ELLIE LAMB AND THE INSTITUTE OF TEXAN CULTURES AT THE UNIVERSITY OF TEXAS AT SAN ANTONIO.

Below: The cornerstone for the current Bexar County Courthouse was laid on December 17, 1892.
COURTESY OF JAMES F. BARTLETT AND THE OFFICE OF COUNTY COMMISSIONER FRANK VAUGHAN, JR.

governing body. It was charged with establishing a courthouse and jail, appointing some county officers, filling some county office vacancies, building and maintaining roads and bridges, and administering public welfare services. It was also responsible for coordinating some elections, setting a county tax rate, issuing bonds, adopting a county budget and serving as a board of equalization for tax assessments.

Above: The Katy Depot in the 1940s. It has since been torn down.

COURTESY OF JOHN AND DELA WHITE AND THE INSTITUTE OF TEXAN CULTURES AT THE UNIVERSITY OF TEXAS AT SAN ANTONIO.

Left: The I.G.& N. Depot in June 1908.

COURTESY OF KELLY MITCHAM AND THE INSTITUTE OF TEXAN CULTURES AT THE UNIVERSITY OF TEXAS AT SAN ANTONIO.

Above: The Plaza de las Islas, around the turn of the twentieth century.
COURTESY OF JAMES F. BARTLETT AND THE OFFICE OF COUNTY COMMISSIONER FRANK VAUGHAN, JR.

Below: The Plaza de las Islas after a second tower was added to San Fernando Cathedral in 1903.
COURTESY OF JAMES F. BARTLETT AND THE OFFICE OF COUNTY COMMISSIONER FRANK VAUGHAN, JR.

Armed with all these new duties, commissioners in Bexar County set out once again to build a new county courthouse. In 1881 a new law permitted the sale of bonds. In 1891, commissioners purchased property on the south side of Plaza de las Islas from Joseph Dwyer and John Kampmann and set up a design competition. The competition was won by a local young man, James Riely Gordon, an architect, and D. E. Laub, with whom he had designed two other courthouses in Texas. He had designed the Texas building at the 1893 World's Columbian Exposition in Chicago and a federal courthouse and post office for San Antonio. The contract to design the new Bexar County Courthouse was the largest commission of his early career. He split from Laub soon after this contract became effective.

The Bexar County building which he designed in the Romanesque Revival Style which became his trademark, has been enlarged several times, making it the largest and most continuously used courthouse in Texas. Gordon designed at least thirteen others in the state which remain standing and several which have been torn down. George Dugan and Otto P. Kroeger won the contract for constructing the new Bexar County Courthouse. The groundbreaking took place on August 4, 1891, and the cornerstone was laid December 17,

1892. Construction required five years and five bond issues. The years of construction were characterized by disputes over foundation workmanship, plumbing and the selection of stone. The initial four-story building and basement was of Texas granite and red sandstone and had an electric elevator. When opened in 1897, it joined the federal courthouse on Alamo Plaza as the largest structures in the county. The east side of the courthouse had protruding wings and a fountain eliminated in later renovations. Various changes were made to the courthouse until 1914, when the H. N. Jones Construction Company implemented a design by Leo M. J. Dielmann and Charles T. Boelhauwe to provide a $75,000 addition from funds provided by a bond issue the year before. A three-story addition was built on the south side of the building.

By 1925 the population of the city alone was pushing 225,000, and the courthouse was crowded. A $2-million bond was floated to once again expand the courthouse. Architects Raymond Phelps, Dahl Dewees, Emmett T. Jackson, and George Willis drew the plans, and Walsh and Burney, Inc., completed the remodeling and addition in two separate contracts. The 1914 addition was partly removed and rebuilt, a fifth story was added over part of the building, and the 1890s building was completely refinished. Green "s-shaped" tile roofing was to become a major feature of the structure.

During the first part of the twentieth century, Bexar County continued as a place on the go. The first bus designed strictly for public use went into operation, but the motorbus was considered a supplement. Streetcar service

The San Antonio City Hall on Military Plaza, c. 1907. The building still is in use as City Hall, after several remodelings.

COURTESY OF JUNE JUMP AND THE INSTITUTE OF TEXAN CULTURES AT THE UNIVERSITY OF TEXAS AT SAN ANTONIO.

Right: The San Antonio Schutzen Verein, a shooting club, c. 1890.

COURTESY OF THE SAN ANTONIO LIGHT COLLECTION, THE INSTITUTE OF TEXAN CULTURES AT THE UNIVERSITY OF TEXAS AT SAN ANTONIO.

Below: The Crockett Hotel, located immediately behind the Alamo, in 1925.

COURTESY OF THE INSTITUTE OF TEXAN CULTURES AT THE UNIVERSITY OF TEXAS AT SAN ANTONIO.

expanded in outlying areas, encouraging suburban growth. In 1923 alone, county citizens logged more than six million miles on streetcars. Not until the next decade was the public bus to become a major factor in mass transit.

The adventures experienced by county residents on mule-drawn streetcars provided many exciting stories of the day—of how businessmen would lift the car from the rails and ask the driver to haul them across the street and over to the Menger Hotel for lunch, for instance. The Menger had been built as a boarding house on Alamo Plaza, just south of the Alamo, in 1855 by William A. Menger and his wife Mary Baumschleuter. The Simon Menger family had established a soap works near San Pedro Creek, the area's major commercial enterprise. In 1857 the William Menger family built a hotel from stone from the Brackenridge Park quarries. They also had opened a brewery, Western Brewery, in 1855. By the 1880s the Menger Hotel had become "the" place to stay, and still is one of the most historic hotels in Texas. Its bar is said to have been a hangout for Teddy Roosevelt and his men, and he purportedly recruited some of the Rough Riders there.

While the Menger brewery operation, run by Charles Degan as brewmaster, was selling yeast from the vats to housewives for a dime a pint, other brewery ventures were starting to form. In

1883, J. B. Behloradsky established the City Brewery on an eight-acre tract along the San Antonio River at River Avenue (now Broadway). It later became known as the San Antonio Brewing Association. In 1894 the general buildings of what became known as Pearl Brewing Company, after its most famous brew, was advertised in newspapers as the largest brewery in the South. In 1887 it produced one hundred thousand kegs, "more than any other brewery south of St. Louis." The manager of the brewery was Otto Koehler, who had arrived in San Antonio in 1883 to manage another brewery which had been formed, Lone Star. That brewery had been established on the river a short distance from the Pearl operation by Adolphus Busch, the St. Louis brewer, and two local businessmen, J. H. Kampmann and G. H. Kalteyer.

Pearl continued to operate at the same location until the spring of 2001. Over the years it had acquired a candy company through a stock swap and several other beer brand names. After Koehler's death in 1969, the brewery was sold several times, including to Jax and Pabst, and the property was cut by a freeway. Today's Pearl property owner, who once owned Pace, a hot sauce firm, is redeveloping the property into a mixed commercial area.

In the meantime, Lone Star closed in 1918. In 1933 another unrelated brewery opened in new quarters on Mission Road, on the south side of the city, at the edge of the roadway connecting the missions. It produced Sabinas and Champion Beer. In 1940, new owners, including Harry Jersig, a name long associated with Lone Star, took over, and began using the name Lone Star Brewing Company. The company recruited a brewmaster from Germany, and he developed a formula for a beer using water from the Edwards Aquifer, the area's

Above: The Menger Hotel, just south of the Alamo, around 1885.
COURTESY OF THE MENGER HOTEL.

Below: The Menger Hotel Bar, an exact replica of London's House of Lords Pub, was where Teddy Roosevelt recruited Rough Riders.
COURTESY OF THE MENGER HOTEL.

Above: Harry Jersig, one of the chief architects of the Lone Star Brewery.
COURTESY OF KATHLEEN JERSIG KUPER.

Right: The original Lone Star Brewing Company, now the San Antonio Museum of Art.
COURTESY OF THE SAN ANTONIO MUSEUM OF ART.

Below: The Pearl Brewery, now being converted into a shopping and residential complex, in the 1910s.
COURTESY OF JOHN AND DELA WHITE AND THE ZINTGRAFF COLLECTION, THE INSTITUTE OF TEXAN CULTURES AT THE UNIVERSITY OF TEXAS AT SAN ANTONIO.

underground supply. Lone Star was advertised as being made from "pure artesian waters" and "the national beer of Texas." Through the years, the Lone Star property, which included a large swimming pool, became a popular place for community gatherings. A wax museum which had been in operation at HemisFair was moved there, as were the properties of the Buckhorn Saloon, a popular central city landmark which had begun operation in 1881, showcasing numerous stuffed animals. Lone Star built a special building for these properties and added a hall of horns. The brewery went through several owners. Lone Star Beer last was brewed in San Antonio by Pabst at the Pearl facility near the turn of the twenty-first century. Jersig's name lives on proudly as that of a speech and hearing center at Our Lady of the Lake University.

Today the old Lone Star property on Jones Avenue south of the old Pearl site has undergone a miraculous era of adaptive reuse as the San Antonio Museum of Art, with the huge and sturdy buildings being an excellent venue for numerous works, including Mexican folkart and Asian works. Unfortunately, the Lone Star property on Mission Road stands abandoned, with nature rapidly taking its toll on a once-active entertainment center and community watering hole.

With Bexar County history so wrapped up in cultural, musical, geographic and economic history, the concept of "fiesta" was bound to play a key role. "Fiesta" is a celebration, a party, complete with all sorts of public festivity. Its Spanish origin is that to honor a saint. The *hijos hidalgos*, the "noble sons," the Canary Islanders who arrived in Bexar County in 1731, first gave rise to the public celebration on January 27, 1747, when they held a week-long party to observe the coronation of a new king of Spain. Kings and queens have been part of Bexar County's annual fiesta celebrations ever since.

In April 1891, on the fifty-fifth anniversary of Sam Houston's victory over the forces of Santa Anna at San Jacinto, the current Fiesta had its origin in one parade. U.S. President Benjamin Harrison was coming to the Alamo City as the first president ever to visit the state, and citizens planned a celebration. Planners for the presidential visit included Ellen Slayden and Mrs. J. S. Alexander. Mrs. Alexander's husband had seen flower parades in Spain and Mexico in which the ladies of the town had "battled" with blossoms, not guns, and a similar parade had been held in Nice, France. Mrs. H. D.

The new Lone Star Brewery, on Mission Road, in the 1950s.

COURTESY OF JOHN AND DELA WHITE AND THE ZINTGRAFF COLLECTION, THE INSTITUTE OF TEXAN CULTURES AT THE UNIVERSITY OF TEXAS AT SAN ANTONIO.

A duchess waves to the crowd during a Battle of Flowers Parade.
COURTESY OF THE FIESTA SAN ANTONIO COMMISSION.

Kampmann was elected chairman of a group which planned a Battle of Flowers Parade in San Antonio, and an association was established to organize the parade. Heavy rains stifled both the parade and the use of flowers in it. The parade had to be postponed because of the rain. The ladies were determined to have the parade anyway and held it later. It included twelve carriages, decorated bicycles, and children dressed as flowers.

The women of the Battle of Flowers Association passed a resolution to hold an observance each year to reflect on the area's past and its heritage and to include the association's parade. For the first five years, the celebration was billed as carnival but was changed to Fiesta to more truly reflect the Spanish roots of the community. And, in 1896, the Battle of Flowers Association sponsored a queen of Fiesta. She was from Austin. The local complaints eventually resulted in the Order of the Alamo, established in 1909, selecting only a San Antonio resident as a Fiesta queen each year. By 1906 the celebration was growing too rapidly for the ladies of the Battle of Flowers to handle alone. Several men had been in the organization, and one had been president, but the women decided to restrict the organization to females only. Also, in 1906, the Spring Carnival Association was formed, and the Battle of Flowers Association became a member. Today, the Battle of Flowers Association is the only all-women organization in the world planning and executing a major parade. They also sponsor a band festival during each year's Fiesta and an oratorical contest to celebrate Texas history. Members wear yellow dresses and hats while supervising their annual parade.

Today the annual Fiesta is coordinated by a commission established by the city, and it includes more than one hundred events celebrating the history of Bexar County. Two other major parades, the Texas Cavaliers' River Parade and the Fiesta Flambeau, have joined the Battle of Flowers Parade. Nearly three million people attend Fiesta events each year, and the economic impact is nearly $254 million.

The first kings of Fiesta were selected by either the Battle of Flowers Association or the San Antonio Chamber of Commerce. They had names such as King Cotton, King Selamat (tamales spelled backwards), King Omala (Alamo spelled backwards) and King Antonio. In 1927, the Texas Cavaliers, a men's equestrian organization formed the previous year, took on the duty of naming a male monarch each year from their ranks, calling him "King Antonio." The first Cavalier king, Sterling Burke, was Antonio IX. The Chamber of Commerce had named the first eight Antonios. In 1980 a second male monarch for Fiesta joined the ranks when *El Rey Feo*, The Ugly King, came from the Spanish tradition where peasants elect one of their own to be king for a day.

One of the most popular Fiesta events continues to be A Night in Old San Antonio, shortened to NIOSA and pronounced, arguably among many, as either NEEosa or NYEosa. It started in 1937 as an Indian festival at Mission San José to raise funds for the preservation work of the San Antonio Conservation Society. The purpose of the event remains the same but the venue is much expanded to La Villita. NIOSA is a festival of food and entertainment which perhaps more than any other event in the city represents the spirit of Fiesta.

Less formal were the activities carried on by San Antonio bawdy houses. David Bowser, in his *San Antonio's Old Red-Light District*, says that at the turn of the twentieth century, San Antonio hosted one of the most-lavish "sporting" areas between New Orleans and San Francisco, an official and legal vice area. In the latter days of the nineteenth century the red-light district had been centered around both Main and Military Plaza in such establishments as Jack Harris' Saloon. It was here that the word "vaudeville" is believed to have found its start. Harris' saloon, the Vaudeville Theater at the corner of Soledad and West Commerce, took on the name "The Fatal Corner," because of the many deadly gunfights which took place there. In July 1882, Harris himself was gunned down there by a former friend, Austin City Marshal Ben Thompson, and a number of famous shootings occurred there later. The customers at such places as the Green

Top, left: Bryan Callaghan was one of three men to have served as both Bexar County judge and mayor of the city.
COURTESY OF THE SAN ANTONIO LIGHT COLLECTION, THE INSTITUTE OF TEXAN CULTURES AT THE UNIVERSITY OF TEXAS AT SAN ANTONIO.

Above: Bryan Callaghan, newly elected mayor of San Antonio for the first time in 1892, celebrates with his friends at the Caroline Kampmann home, now the site of the city's Willow Springs Golf Club. With Callaghan (fourth from left) are William "Pap" Page, a famous fisherman and sportsman of the day; Jones Irwin; Hermann Kampmann, Sr., owner of the Menger Hotel; Frank Mason; and James Simpson (seated).
COURTESY OF THE INSTITUTE OF TEXAN CULTURES AT THE UNIVERSITY OF TEXAS AT SAN ANTONIO.

Below: Teddy Roosevelt, in the right rear seat of this open touring car in April 1905, was in Bexar County for a reunion of the Rough Riders. The man next to him is Bryan Callaghan, about to return to the mayorship. John S. Campbell, the former mayor, is one of the men in front of Callaghan.
COURTESY OF THE SAN ANTONIO EXPRESS-NEWS AND THE INSTITUTE OF TEXAN CULTURES AT THE UNIVERSITY OF TEXAS AT SAN ANTONIO.

Front Saloon and the Silver King Saloon were drovers off the cattle trails, soldiers, gamblers, gunfighters, and some merchants—perhaps even Texas Rangers.

To the east, on the other side of the Alamo, at the corner of Elm and Starr, Blanche Dearwood had been operating a bawdy house since the 1870s. Her "Fort Allen," so named because its thick adobe walls and steep roof made it look fortress-like, had nothing official about it. Sometime in the 1880s the red-light district became centered in a tract a few blocks west of Military Plaza, the site of City Hall, and south and west to Market Square. The region, called "West of the Creek" (San Pedro Creek crossed Commerce just west of City Hall), had been platted by City Engineer Francois Giraud in 1849 but it generally had been uninhabited because of raids by Native Americans. Up until 1879 those seen mostly in the area were wagon freighters coming up from Mexico.

During 1889-1890, in the reign of Mayor Bryan Callaghan, a machine politician (he also was a Bexar County judge), the city fathers officially laid out a fifteen-block red-light district. This district was bounded by just south of Market Square at Dolorosa Street, three blocks south to Durango Street and south along Santa Rosa Street and five blocks west to Frio Street near the railroad yards. These establishments operated under a general "understanding" until the outbreak of World War II in 1941. The glory days of the district were from 1890 to 1920, with more than 100 brothels listed in Billy Kielman's 1911-1912 *Blue Book*, a guide to entertainment in the area. Some of the most famous madams, including Lillian Revere, Marguerite Clifford, and Sallie Brewer, ran advertisements in the book. Refugees from the Mexican Revolution, plotting an overthrow of the government south of the border, were frequent customers. All of this was taking place within sight of both the county courthouse and City Hall on one side and the Catholic Santa Rosa hospital on the other. Milam Park was the Protestant cemetery in the area, and the Catholic cemetery was located where Santa Rosa now stands. When the hospital was built, the bodies were moved to the west side of the county to San Fernando Cemetery No. 1.

But east and north of the courthouse there were some developments going on which added great value, not debauchery, to the history of the

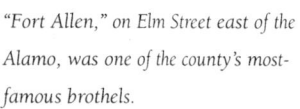

"Fort Allen," on Elm Street east of the Alamo, was one of the county's most-famous brothels.

COURTESY OF THE SAN ANTONIO EXPRESS-NEWS AND THE SAN ANTONIO LIGHT COLLECTION, THE INSTITUTE OF TEXAN CULTURES AT THE UNIVERSITY OF TEXAS AT SAN ANTONIO.

area. These were developments that would close out the Golden Age of Bexar with a new, an uncertain, day coming. The first was the construction downtown of the Milam Building, which in 1928 became the tallest reinforced concrete and the first fully air-conditioned building in the United States. It remains today as one of the city's major office structures.

The second was the construction of the Smith-Young Tower. It opened in June 1929 after the river was straightened and filled in around former Bowen's Island, which had been a favorite garden spot, swimming hole and entertainment area. The 35-story building, designed by Atlee and Robert Ayres as an adjunct to the 250-room Plaza Hotel across the street (the buildings were joined by an underground tunnel), was until the 1950s, one of the tallest buildings west of the Mississippi and is one of the very few octagonal buildings in the world. The building, which housed the city's first Sears store and later became known as the Transit Tower, as the bus system was headquartered there, now is the Tower Life Building and is an insurance headquarters. Other buildings from the same era are Alamo National Bank, The Nix Building, and Frost Bank.

Above The Milam Building, c. 1928, was the largest all-concrete and first air conditioned office building in the nation.
COURTESY OF THE SAN ANTONIO EXPRESS-NEWS AND THE INSTITUTE OF TEXAN CULTURES AT THE UNIVERSITY OF TEXAS AT SAN ANTONIO.

Top, left: The Smith-Young Tower, now the Tower Life Building, opened in 1929.
COURTESY OF JAMES ZACHRY, TOWER LIFE INSURANCE COMPANY.

Bottom, left: La Villita, home to many early citizens of Bexar County.

Chapter V ◆ 87

CHAPTER VI

INTO SUBURBIA

Even though Bexar County went through extensive agricultural mechanization, including for pecan shelling, the 1930s Depression hit the county hard. Farm prices fell, and cotton production plummeted as the boll weevil found a new home. Had it not been for government works projects, including restoration on the river, the job market would have been nil.

San Antonio lost to Dallas its place as the state's largest city and failed to become the home of Texas' largest Centennial celebration. Nevertheless, there were bright spots and significant changes. In 1933 the Alamo City became the first large city in the nation to abandon electric street cars, giving way to the motorized bus. The city took over the gas and electric system in 1942, but auctioned off the bus system to the privately owned San Antonio Transit Company. That company struggled for many years but in 1947 placed in service fifty of the world's first air-conditioned buses. The city took the system over in 1959 as the San Antonio Transit System and voters in 1977 approved the creation of VIA Metropolitan Transit as the first regional transit authority in the nation, funded by a local half-cent sales tax. Today, VIA, a state agency, rather than a city or county department, remains one of the best-operated mass transit systems in the nation. Its nearly 500 buses serve 99 percent of Bexar County, including San Antonio and 14 suburban cities, plus three suburbs at the edge of the county.

Freeway planning began in Bexar County in 1943. The first section of Interstate 10, from Woodlawn Avenue to Martin Street, opened in 1951. In 1956 the first section of Interstate 35, from Alamo Street to Broadway, opened, and the first section of Loop 410 opened in 1957. Today, Bexar County has 161.138 miles of interstate highway, 74.87 miles of U.S. highway, 221.95 miles of state highway, 179.87 miles of farm-to-market or ranch-to-market roadway, 6.69 miles of park road, and 331.97 miles of frontage road.

From 1941 to 1944 the land for an airport in north Bexar was purchased, and the first terminal of San Antonio International Airport opened in 1953. As the city grew, other airport facilities were needed. The city expanded the terminal in 1959 and completed a satellite gate area and hold rooms to serve the influx of visitors for HemisFair '68. The city adopted an airport master plan in 1975 to provide for facilities through 2000. In 1982 a new thirteen-hundred-space, tri-level parking garage was constructed and the city completed a second terminal two years later. The city built a new FAA air traffic control tower in 1986 to replace the one installed in 1953. In 1988 the city built an airport fire/rescue station, the largest fire station in San Antonio. In the 1990s the city built new runways, adopted a noise compatibility program for the airport, and insulated nearby neighborhood public buildings against noise intrusion. It also implemented a new twenty-year master plan, built a new five-story long-term parking garage, and developed a plan for terminal renovation and concession redevelopment. In 2001 the aviation department opened the 281 North Connector, which provides direct elevated access from U.S. 281 North into the terminal and parking facilities. All of these expansions were to meet increased air travel to accommodate the nation's ninth largest city. Much of the county's private air operations have shifted to Stinson Field in South Bexar County.

The cultural infrastructure also has been key to the development of Bexar County. A major plus for the local arts community occurred in 1930 when the San Pedro Playhouse opened in San Pedro Park, to carry on the productions of the San Antonio Little Theater. The façade of the playhouse is a reproduction of the Old Market House, which had been built just east of Plaza de las Islas in 1858 but was razed in 1925 to make way for a street widening. The actual pillars from the market complex were supposed to be used on the new arts structure, but unthinking workmen had dumped them in a trash heap. The unsuccessful effort to save the old Market House was among the first efforts of the San Antonio Conservation Society. The opening of the new theater was momentous because of the crowd which attended, led by the mayor. It also was noteworthy because fire engines, ambulances, emergency

Opposite: Early mass transportation in Bexar County.
COURTESY OF VIA METROPOLITAN TRANSIT.

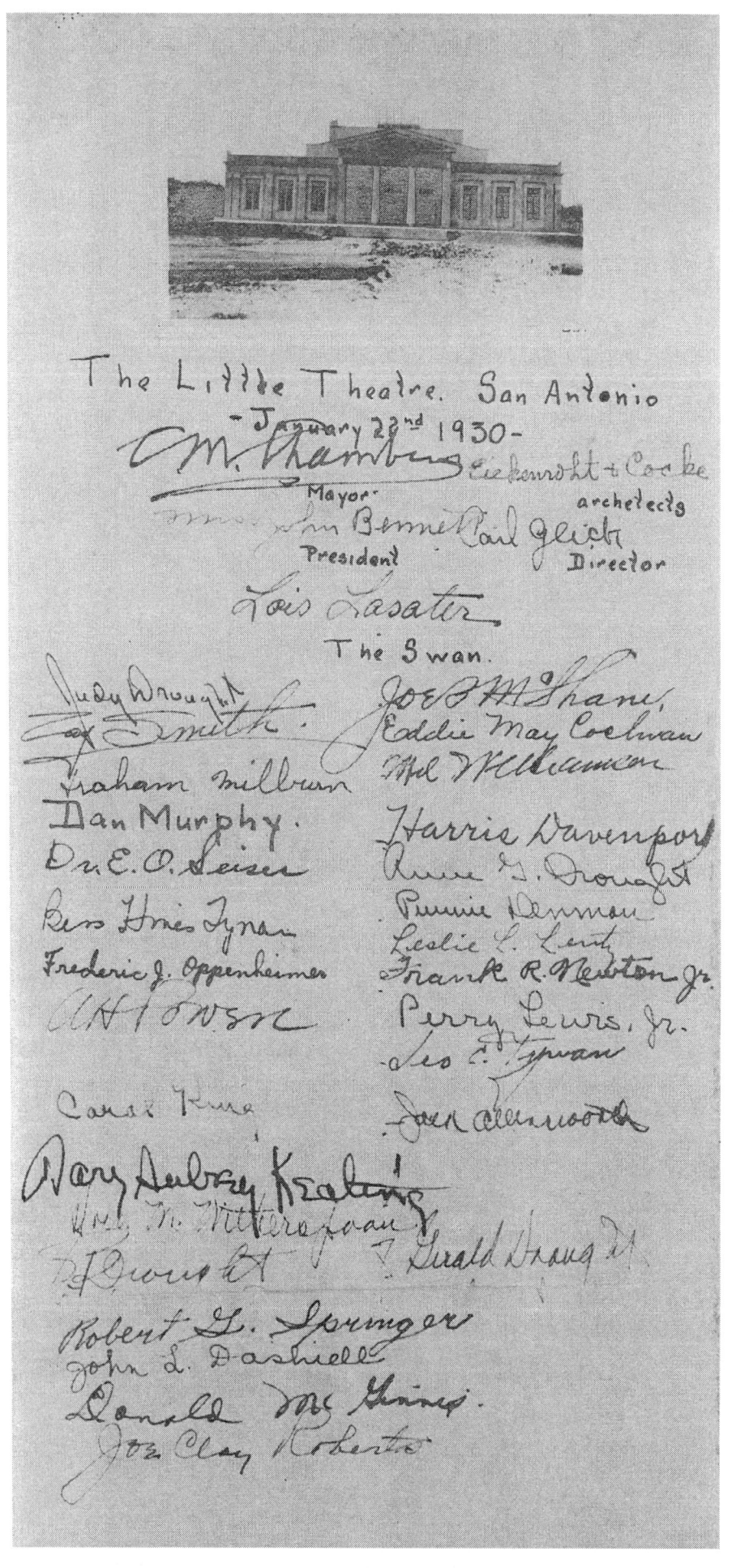

vehicles, and fire extinguisher-handling firemen were on hand, as the new building had no fire inspection certificate and the fire chief had threatened to shut down the opening play, *The Swan*.

On March 22, 1924, the San Antonio Conservation Society had been founded, specifically to save the Old Market House east of Main Plaza. The organization's general purpose, however, was to keep the physical and cultural heritage of San Antonio. Even though the organization was started by a group of women who favored the arts more than structure, the Conservation Society has come to be the county's most important conduit for preserving historic buildings. In that vein the group early took on the task of saving the river, especially its river bend, from being filled in. Even though they lost the fight to save the Market House, its columns, entablature and pediment were replicated for the San Pedro Playhouse. The society, as early as its year of founding, approached city and county leaders on river improvements. The society also joined with Adina de Zavala to save the Spanish Governor's Palace. Perhaps more than any other organization in Bexar County, the Conservation Society, with its three thousand members, represents the community awareness of the importance of history in San Antonio. Bexar County has a large number of highly qualified "citizen historians." Reflected in its efforts to save the river and the River Walk, the missions or little-known historical buildings under threat of the wrecking ball, the Conservation Society maintains one chief strategy: Demand that all be saved in order to save the best.

The elements of the arts community in Bexar historically have had a close, but often competitive, relationship, as various organizations formed. The San Antonio Art League came about in 1912 as the oldest of the organizations. Through the years its collection has been housed at the Frost Bank; at the Municipal Auditorium, built to commemorate the heroes of World War I, and at the Witte Museum. It also has used venues at the McNay Art Museum, originally Sunset Hills, the home of Marion Koogler McNay; at the Belgian Pavilion at HemisFair Plaza; and at the League's current location, the Scheer House in the King William District.

Opposite: The playbill for the opening of the Little Theatre in San Pedro Park on January 22, 1930, was signed by the mayor, C. M. Chambers, theater officials, and cast members. The production was The Swan.
COURTESY OF THE SAN ANTONIO LITTLE THEATER

Left: The San Antonio Art League Museum, the area's oldest arts organization, is in the King William District.
COURTESY OF THE SAN ANTONIO ART LEAGUE MUSEUM.

Below: The McNay Art Museum originally was the home of Marion Koogler McNay.
COURTESY OF THE MCNAY ART MUSEUM LIBRARY & ARCHIVES, SAN ANTONIO, TEXAS.

The McNay was opened in 1954 in north Bexar as the first museum of modern art in Texas. In 1929 the Witte Museum started as a natural history facility, but today has been expanded to include permanent collections highlighting the human development and scientific background of Texas. In 2004 it was one of the few venues for the traveling "American Originals: Treasures from the National Archives" exhibit. The H-E-B Science Treehouse at the Witte is one of the most-popular field trip spots for Bexar County students. The San Antonio Museum of Art in the old Lone Star Brewery continues to expand with wings for specialized collections.

While the McNay, the Witte and the San Antonio Museum of Art continue to be the county's most-popular museum outlets, area citizens have had the opportunity to enjoy a variety of facilities which have spotlighted the community's diverse ethnic makeup in cultural arts settings. The Guadalupe Theater, built in 1940, was a landmark in the county's western sector with its neon-encircled spire rising above a cobalt blue and pumpkin orange exterior. In 1984 the historic theater became part of the Guadalupe Cultural Arts Center, one of the premier Latino community-based arts organizations in the nation. It is dedicated to preserving the culture of the area's Latino/Chicano/indigenous peoples through

Above: The housewarming/formal opening of Sunset Hills, Marion Koogler McNay's Sunset Hills, which later became the McNay Art Museum, drew a large crowd of prominent local citizens on June 10, 1930.
COURTESY OF THE MCNAY ART MUSEUM LIBRARY & ARCHIVES, SAN ANTONIO, TEXAS.

Below: The H-E-B Science Treehouse at the Witte Museum is a favorite of area youngsters.

dance, music, literature, and media, visual, and theater arts. Another artistic complex in the county is the Blue Star, opened in a warehouse area at the edge of the King William District.

In March 1949 the Alameda Theater near the center of the city was the largest theater palace ever built for Spanish-language entertainment. Located in the International Building, the twenty-four-hundred-seat art deco theater was built by cinema magnate G. A. Lucchese as "a permanent symbol of good faith and understanding between the Latin-American and Anglo-American." The city-owned Alameda has been incorporated into a plan to revitalize the western end of the city's downtown area through its use in conjunction with the John F. Kennedy Center for the Performing Arts and a Smithsonian-affiliated museum two blocks away in Market Square.

In 1903 a branch library for African-American citizens of San Antonio opened in a room at the Riverside Colored High School. African-American leaders organized the Colored Library Association shortly thereafter to improve the library for the community. In 1914 the George Washington Carver Branch Library opened on North Hackberry to serve African-American U.S. Army personnel. In 1929, this library, located in the Colored Community House, was torn down and replaced the following year by Carver Library Auditorium. Such well-known artists as Ella Fitzgerald, Lionel Hampton, Paul Robeson, Louis Armstrong, Dizzie Gillespie, Cab Calloway, and Billy Eckstein preformed there. Such noted entertainers came to the county at times without the notice of the Anglo population. The center was closed in the late 1960s and was threatened with demolition that was avoided because of significant public opposition including citizens lying down in front of the bulldozer. In 1977 the city opened the renovated Carver Community Cultural Center and moved the library two miles to the east. It was closed again in 2000, but reopened in mid-2004 after a $3.6-million renovation. It is now part of a complex which includes another performing arts building. Sharing this culture campus is the Carver Academy, a school founded by former San Antonio Spurs basketball great David Robinson. As some cultural services were provided under Carver auspices as early as 1905, the Carver will celebrate its centennial in 2005. Cary Clack, a columnist for the *San Antonio Express-News*, wrote, "What the Apollo Theater means to Harlem, the Carver Community Cultural Center means to the East Side of San Antonio." Another well-known East Side cultural icon structure went by the way of progress several decades ago. The Eastwood Country Club's house band and comedians supported national and local headliners.

The Guadalupe Theater opened in 1940.
COURTESY OF THE GUADALUPE CULTURAL ARTS CENTER.

Left: The Alameda Theater opened in 1949 as the largest theater ever built for Spanish-language entertainment.
COURTESY OF THE ALAMEDA THEATER.

Right: A Richard Q. Kroninger photo of the old dormitory building of the Ursuline Academy, with its three-faced clock tower, now part of the Southwest School of Art & Craft.
COURTESY OF THE SOUTHWEST SCHOOL OF ART & CRAFT.

One of the county's chief cultural institutions continues to struggle with funding and diversification of public support. German immigrants brought symphonic music played to Bexar audiences as early as the 1850s. The San Antonio Symphony, an excellent musical organization which began in 1939, cancelled the latter part of its 2003 season but will have a 2004-2005 season.

Another of the long-time entertainment venues, formed initially in Brackenridge Park in 1942, but established more permanently at Broadway and Alamo the next year, was Playland Park. The park, especially noted for its carousel and roller coaster, closed in 1986. Just a few blocks north on Broadway, Kiddie Park, opened in 1925 with a small roller coaster and rides for youngsters, continues to operate in aging facilities. That does not seem to trouble grandparents who played there when they were children, and now watch their grandkids' happy smiles in the park.

Also surviving were such well-known hotels as the St. Anthony and the Gunter. The first, built on Travis Park in 1909, became the first air-conditioned hotel in the nation. The latter, constructed the same year at Houston and St. Mary's streets on the site which had been the Bexar headquarters for both the U. S. Army and the Confederacy, and later, the Mahncke Hotel, had become famous as a headquarters for visiting cattlemen. Houston Street had become the city's "main street" around 1899.

Lost to antiquity by the mid-1950s were most of the theaters which had become favorite outing places for families and those neighborhood movie palaces for our youth—the Harlandale, the Highlands, the Laurel, the Broadway, the Uptown, the Olmos, the State, the Palace, and the Woodlawn. The Broadway, in Alamo Heights, became an office building, and the Woodlawn, where John Wayne's *The Alamo* premiered, remained a while as both a movie theater and a performing arts theater. Some of the county's various drive-in theaters held on for a longer time, enjoying a heyday in the 1950s. One still operates on Roosevelt Avenue. It was these places where Roy Rogers and Gene Autry were the kings of the screen and *Jack Armstrong*, *Sky King*, *Hopalong Cassidy*, and the *Durango Kid* were serials at all-day Saturday matinees. What a blow it was to the family budget when the admission went from nine cents to a quarter! Some of the movie houses survived. The elegant Majestic on Houston and the Charline McCombs Empire just around the corner (and connected to the Majestic by back stage) became palaces of performing arts under the guidance of Joci Straus (Mrs. Joe Straus, Jr.) and the Las Casas Foundation. The nearby Aztec remains dark, awaiting long-promised

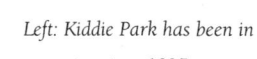

Left: Kiddie Park has been in operation since 1925.

Below: Paul McSween, as manager of the Gunter Hotel, registers movie star Tom Mix and his horse at the room check-in about 1930.
COURTESY OF PAUL MCSWEEN, JR.

redevelopment. The Josephine Street Theatre now holds theatrical performances.

Many businesses have been able to survive in a newer age. One is the L. Frank Saddlery Company, formed in the late years of the nineteenth century to provide goods for those traveling the Western and Chisholm Trails. The company initially was on Alamo Plaza, but moved several times, once to the Karotkin Building on Commerce, now being converted into a hotel. The company became quite famous for the creation of miniature saddles, one of which was given to U.S. President Ronald Reagan by the National Association of Manufacturers. Company catalogs

Above: The Aztec Theater, known for its unusual design, now is vacant.
COURTESY OF THE ZINTGRAFF COLLECTION, THE INSTITUTE OF TEXAN CULTURES AT THE UNIVERSITY OF TEXAS AT SAN ANTONIO.

Right: The Broadway Theater now is an office building.

carried a phrase, "Horse, next to woman, God's greatest gift to man," aimed to forestall the replacement of the horse by the automobile. A book telling the story of the company carries that title. Eventually, the firm changed its name to the Straus-Frank Company, moved to a site at the southern edge of downtown San Antonio and became, ironically, among other things, a major distributor of auto parts.

Unfortunately, following a disturbing national trend, Bexar County has but one daily newspaper, the *San Antonio Express-News*. It was founded in 1865 and today ranks in circulation (Sunday, 356,400; daily, 234,875) 35th among the 1,600 daily newspapers in the nation. The Hearst Corporation in January 1993 closed its own paper, the *San Antonio Light*, which had been formed in 1881, after Hearst purchased the *Express-News* from Australian Rupert Murdoch. *La Prensa*, a publication in Spanish and English, was formed to serve the refugees of the Mexican Revolution of 1910. It publishes twice a week. The area has a number of weekly newspapers. One of the leading weekly subscription papers is the *North San Antonio Times*, owned by Prime Time Newspapers, a company which also publishes the area military newspapers. Other regional papers in the county, including papers in towns like Helotes, provide free distribution to their readers.

In the late 1940s a development came about which proved to be both a temporary and a permanent advantage of county and city cooperation in Bexar. The county had seen its first agricultural fair in 1854, on exposition grounds in the far east area of the county, and Bexar always had outstanding agriculture and livestock production. In 1945 the city handed over 175 acres in the area for the construction of the Joe and Harry Freeman Coliseum. County Judge Charles W. Anderson proposed the new facility, designed by a group called the Coliseum Architects

composed of Bartlett Cocke, Raymond Phelps, Dahl DeWees, Simmons, and Atlee B. and Robert Ayres. To set the building apart from politics, all income from the use of the facility itself was dedicated to scholarships under the guidance of an appointed civic board. County commissioners appointed the first board. In 1949 the first San Antonio Stock Show and Rodeo was held at the new Coliseum, entertaining more than a quarter million visitors, an unheard of record for an opening show. Since then the San Antonio Livestock Exposition has hosted the stock show at the site and operated an aggressive program of agricultural education, especially for the young people of the area. Recently the Exposition has moved into the new SBC Center.

One of the major factors making Bexar County ripe for the beginning and continued success of a

Above: Among the features on Alamo Plaza in the late nineteenth century was L. Frank Saddlery Company.
COURTESY OF DAVID STRAUS, STRAUS-FRANK COMPANY.

Below: The Joe and Harry Freeman Coliseum was built as a joint government venture in the late 1940s.
COURTESY OF THE SAN ANTONIO LIVESTOCK EXPOSITION.

Chapter VI ♦ 97

Above: The Joe and Harry Freeman Coliseum today.
COURTESY OF THE BEXAR COUNTY COLISEUM OFFICE.

Below: Our Lady of Mt. Carmel Church at El Carmen, near Losoya in south Bexar County, c. 1900.
COURTESY OF CARMELA RAMOS FERRER AND THE INSTITUTE OF TEXAN CULTURES AT UTSA.

major stock show was the development of a highly successful network of suburban cities in the county. Many of them had strong agricultural roots, and supplement the diversity of San Antonio. The arrival of the railroad in the 1870s had been responsible for the development of many urban communities in the county, well-known areas such as Macdona, Von Ormy, Cassin, Thelma and Losoya. Most of these communities sprang up in the southern part of the county, and few of them ever became incorporated cities.

Cassin was the home to a well-known area store, started in 1913 by August Charles (A. C.) Toudouze. His grandparents, Josephine and Gustave Toudouze, had left France in 1848 and opened a gift shop and museum in the Grenet Store, on the grounds of the Alamo. In 1916, Toudouze moved from Cassin fifteen miles north into San Antonio and opened a store at the intersection of Pleasanton Road and South Flores Street, complete with a lumber yard and the area's first customer parking lot. Over the years, the Toudouze interests continued to flourish, beginning the area's first cash-and-carry warehouse. Now, members of the third generation of Toudouzes operate the Toudouze Market, carrying more than six thousand items of food and supplies.

Some of the subdivisions actually within the San Antonio limits are sometimes treated as if they are suburbs. These include Monte Vista, an area developed during the early years of the twentieth century and the home of the cattle barons, and the gated communities of the Dominion and Elm Creek, where many of the residents are the recently affluent of the community.

Besides such communities as Macdona, Von Ormy, Cassin, Thelma, and Losoya which had been developed in the county, but are not incorporated cities with their own municipal structure, there are many others. These include Adkins, Atascosa, Berg's Mill, Boldtville, Buena Vista, Fratt, Kirk, Idelwilde, Lande (Luxello), Locke Hill, Lone Oak, San Lucas Springs, Mangus Corner, Maun's Crossing, Midway, Oak Island, Martinez, Pareta, Saunders, Sayers, Senior, Southtown, Terrell Wells, and Wetmore. La Coste is an incorporated area, but it is in nearby Medina County, barely touching the Bexar County line. Some of these communities still are listed on the 2003 Bexar County Major Thoroughfares map of MAPSCO, Inc.

Left: The Gustave Toudouze home in the Cassin-Losoya area in south Bexar County, c. 1870. The Toudouze family built a well-known Bexar County business.

COURTESY OF CHARLES TOUDOUZE AND THE INSTITUTE OF TEXAN CULTURES AT THE UNIVERSITY OF TEXAS AT SAN ANTONIO.

Below: This is the new entrance being dug by spelunkers for Robber Baron Cave, one of 494 caves in Bexar County.

What evolved eventually in a governmentally official way was a Bexar County made up of a central city, one of the largest in the nation, and 24 incorporated cities, all but three completely within the confines of the county. Some of the suburban cities are close in, engulfed by San Antonio.

Here are the stories of the incorporated suburban cities: (the populations reflect the 2000 U.S. Census)

ALAMO HEIGHTS
POPULATION: 7,319

This is the oldest incorporated suburb in the county. In 1839, development in the area at the headwaters of the San Antonio River first was called the "City of Avoca." In 1852, San Antonio Alderman J. S. Sweet built his home, "Sweet Homestead," at the headwaters. In 1858, Charles Anderson built a horse ranch headquarters at the edge of Olmos Basin and later sold it to H. H. McLane; in 1890, McLane sold out to a Denver firm. The local agents of the Denver firm, Charles Ogden, R. H. Russell, and J. W. B. Patterson, named the Anderson mansion the "Argyle," (Patterson said the area reminded him of his native Argyleshire) and made it into a hotel. It now is a private club owned by the Southwest Foundation for Biomedical Research. George Brackenridge had built his home on the Sweet land, calling his

Chapter VI ♦ 99

entire estate Alamo Heights. On Christmas Day 1900, the Alamo Heights Land and Development Company began homesites, and nearby areas called Montclair and Madeleine Terrace were opened in 1907-1908. Collectively the entire area soon was called Alamo Heights, and it was incorporated as such at a ceremony on the lawn of the Argyle in 1922. The City Hall opened on Broadway in 1927, and "Bluebonnet Hills" was annexed in 1928 and "Sylvan Hills" in 1944. Even though many of the homes in Alamo Heights are of a 1920s cottage style, it is one of the "Tri Cities," along with Olmos Park and Terrell Hills, close-in suburbs which have some of the most palatial homes in the county.

BALCONES HEIGHTS
POPULATION: 3,022

This suburb in the northwest section of the county takes its name from an escarpment named Los Balcones by the Spanish in the 1750s, as the land resembled a series of balconies. Major home development in the area started in the early 1930s, after the completion of the nearby Jefferson High School in San Antonio, spurred by promotional competition between two companies. In a swirl of controversy over ways to control zoning and keep San Antonio from annexing the area, Balcones Heights incorporated in 1948. San Antonio Mayor Gus Mauerman had led an unsuccessful legal fight to de-incorporate Alamo Heights, Olmos Park, and Terrell Hills, in the fight to extend the limits of San Antonio around these three cities and increase San Antonio's area by sixty-eight percent. On the south side of the county a plan to incorporate the City of Terrell Wells failed. When Balcones Heights did not have enough money to repair its streets, a WPA-like program was begun to require all males between the ages of 21 and 45 (preachers excepted) to give five days of public service each year to the city. One could make a financial contribution for exemption, however. After years of financial struggles, the state sales tax brought a bonanza to Balcones Heights as Wonderland Shopping Center, now Crossroads Mall, was established in the 1960s. Some even

Looking toward the intersection of Patterson Avenue and Torcido Drive in Alamo Heights, near the headwaters of the San Antonio River, c. 1900.

COURTESY OF THE SAN ANTONIO LIGHT COLLECTION, THE INSTITUTE OF TEXAN CULTURES AT UNIVERSITY OF TEXAS AT SAN ANTONIO.

advocated, unsuccessfully, to rename the town Wonderland. Today, Balcones Heights remains one of the smallest in land of the county's suburbs, but its density is by far the greatest, with more than half its land in commercial development and eighty percent of the residents living in apartments.

CASTLE HILLS
POPULATION: 4,200

This city in the north section of the county was carved out of farm, ranch and dairy land owned by the Prinz, Slimp, Manton, and Finck families. The name Castle Hills came from the home of Chester Slimp, Jr. His two-story rock home on the highest elevation in the area had been called, "the castle on the hill." Under a cloud of possible annexation, it was incorporated in 1951 and eventually called the "City of Beautiful Homes." The City of San Antonio attempted to overturn the incorporation but was unsuccessful. In 2004, Castle Hills led the development of The North Corridor Association of cities that included seven suburban cities. The purpose was to work on problems of mutual interest.

CHINA GROVE
POPULATION: 1,247

This town in the eastern section of the county was incorporated in 1960. It is the subject of a song, *China Grove*, recorded by the Doobie Brothers.

CONVERSE
POPULATION: 12,000

This town in the northeast section of the county began development in the early years of the twentieth century and was organized under a home rule charter in 1981. It is the home of the Judson High School Rockets, six times the Texas State Division 5A football champions and is at the southwestern edge of Randolph Air Force Base. Converse has seen phenomenal growth. From 1970 to 1980, the area's population grew by 254 percent. By 2010, Converse is expected to have a population well beyond twenty thousand.

ELMENDORF
POPULATION: 750

This town in southern Bexar County is named for the Elmendorf family and was incorporated in 1963. Carl Alexander "Charles" Elmendorf came from Germany in the middle of the nineteenth century, settling first in New Braunfels and then coming to San Antonio. His family was opposed to secession, moving first to Mexico and then back to Germany during the Civil War. He returned his family to San Antonio in 1866 and opened a hardware store on Plaza de las Islas. He also opened a brick factory in south Bexar County, and the Elmendorf name became associated with brick making. Charles Elmendorf's son, Henry, was mayor of San Antonio in 1895.

FAIR OAKS RANCH
POPULATION: 4,695

This is one of the youngest towns in Texas, having been incorporated in 1988. Ralph E. Fair, Sr., had accumulated properties in the

Crossroads Shopping Mall, formerly Wonderland, is the shopping city that built the Bexar County suburban city of Balcones Heights.

1930s, 1940s, and 1950s in far northwest Bexar County and two adjoining counties, including the land which was formed into a town. The Fair heirs had developed a golf and country club there.

GREY FOREST
POPULATION: 418

The area of this town, in western Bexar County, was developed in 1929 as Scenic Loop Playground and was a favorite place of relaxation, especially after World War II. When the City of San Antonio made overtures to annex the area and turn it into a park or zoo, the residents incorporated the town in 1962.

HELOTES
POPULATION: 4,285

This town, also in scenic hills in the western section of the county, was the home of Lipan Apaches and draws its name from *helote*, or corn, which was the major crop for Native Americans. Today's Cornyval, a festival held each May in Helotes, is an outgrowth of the Apache practice of celebrating after the corn was ripe. Helotes became a major stagecoach stop between San Antonio and Bandera, and an area to its west became known as "Hillotes." Mary Lee Gussen Sloan gives a vivid 1850s account of life in the Helotes and surrounding area, including northwest San Antonio in the Culebra Road section, in her *And the Snake Slept*. This book shows how much the farming families of Bexar County, so much like the ranching families of South Texas, exercised an interdependence that kept progress coming.

HILL COUNTRY VILLAGE
POPULATION: 1,038

This north Bexar County town was formed from a portion of the homesteaded land adjacent to the Coker Ranch, which dates from the republic period of Texas. Later, hogs on a farm in the middle of the area were fed from garbage from Fort Sam Houston, and the military developed a trail through the area into Camp Bullis. Portions of the trail, used by horse riders today, still are visible in Artisans Alley on Bitters Road. A waterworks was formed there following World War II and the area incorporated in 1956, when the City of San Antonio was moving toward annexing the area. Hill Country Village remains a town of rural character, with large homes on large tracts of land.

HOLLYWOOD PARK
POPULATION: 2,983

Named for the California horse racing track, this town is bordered on the south by Hill Country Village and on the north by Loop 1604. It was incorporated in December 1955 and has a town-owned recreation area, which includes a swimming pool and tennis courts. Free ranging deer have been a major problem for this community.

KIRBY
POPULATION: 8,673

Kirby was a railroad town which continued to grow after the major rail traffic had left, although a major rail yard for maintenance of engines and freight cars still exists. The town began development in the 1920s, grew after Randolph Air Force Base came in to its north, and was incorporated in May 1955. Clara Weller, in her "scrapbook" called *My Town: Kirby*, gives the story of the families who settled in the town.

LEON VALLEY
POPULATION: 9,239

This area, in northwest Bexar, once was populated by Lipan Apaches and Comanches. Early on, the area was known as "Huebner Settlement," after German settler Joseph Huebner, who, in 1862, built a home on the current State Highway 16 to Bandera. That home and stage stop now is being developed into a living museum by the Historical Society of Leon Valley. The town, faced by possible annexation by San Antonio, was incorporated in 1952. The town's name comes from Leon Creek, a tributary of the Medina River, and recognizes that mountain lions once roamed the area (*león* is the Spanish word for "lion," and the Native Americans called the area the "Valley of the Lions"). Leon Valley is in one of the fastest growing areas of the county, as the gateway to the Sea World and Fiesta Texas Six Flags amusements parks nearby. A popular Leon Valley attraction is Raymond Rimkus Park, named for the city's first mayor.

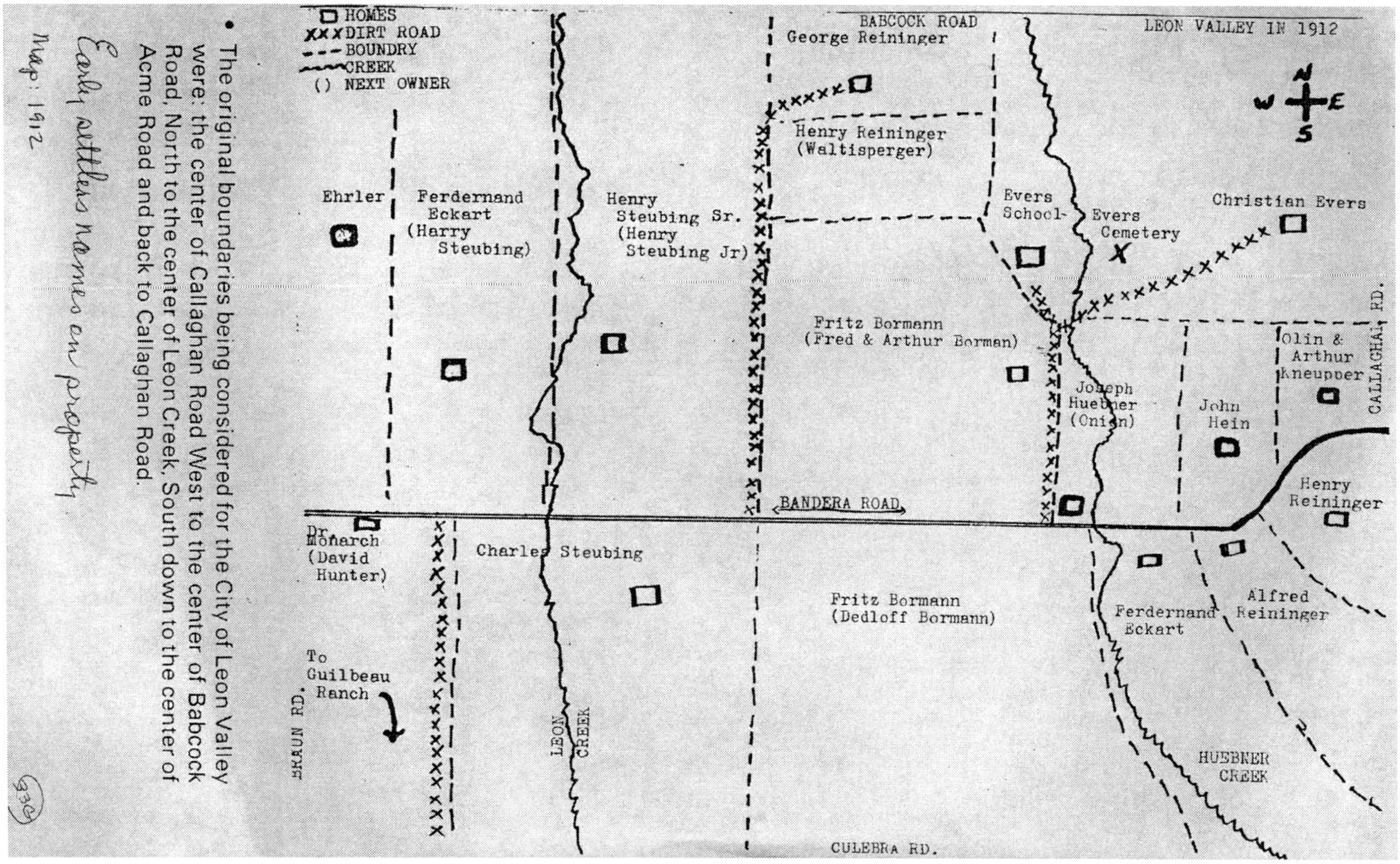

LIVE OAK
POPULATION: 9,156

Some residents of this town, on the northern edge of San Antonio on the highway to Austin and the cutoff to Randolph Air Force Base, initially lived within Selma, another town just to its north. In 1957, the old German cotton farming com-munity of Selma incorporated. Due to many disagreements, the town unincorporated in 1958. Two years later, the residents in the southern section of old Selma met under a live oak tree and incorporated the City of Live Oak. Later in the decade, the town took in nearby Pan American Speedway, which had been built by Jimmy Johnson, who also owned Playland Park in San Antonio. The speedway closed in 1979. In 1980-81, Live Oak won a legal battle with San Antonio to take in nearby Woodcrest and Robards.

LYTLE
POPULATION: 2,383

This is a railroad town formed in 1882, and only a small portion of it lies within southwestern Bexar County. Most of Lytle is in Atascosa County, with a portion in Medina County. The town became incorporated in 1951. It has both a city park and a country club.

OLMOS PARK
POPULATION: 2,343

This is one of the "Tri-Cities," forming an affluent area of the county with Alamo Heights and Terrell Hills quite close in to the north central area of San Antonio and surrounded by the City of San Antonio. In the early 1920s the area was called Uhjazzi, as Char Miller and Heywood T. Sanders wrote in "Olmos Park and the Creation of a Suburban Bastian, 1927-39" in *Urban Texas*, "a small reminder of European

A 1912 map showing the locations of some of the properties of the early familes on Leon Valley, a suburban Bexar County town.

COURTESY OF THE CITY OF LEON VALLEY.

The Olmos Pharmacy, at the edge of Olmos Park, has one of the few oldtime soda fountains still left in Bexar County. Note the historic misspelling of Olmos on the top of the clock.

grace in South Texas." In the late nineteenth century, Ladislaus Uhjazzi, a European count, had built an elaborate mansion there. Herman Charles Thorman, who had come from Ohio and then made his fortune in the Luling oil fields, developed neighborhoods in the Highlands area in southeast San Antonio, in the Fredericksburg Road area and Country Club Estates south of the San Antonio Country Club.

In the 1920s he purchased land in Uhjazzi and began development of Olmos Park Estates. It was a city planned much like Highland Park in Dallas and River Oaks in Houston, with restrictions on ethnicity and size of lots, houses and price on homes. Thorman's new property lay just west of Olmos Basin, and when Olmos Dam was finished in 1927 his new subdivision was of great advantage, as the new roadway across the dam provided a link to Olmos Park Estates between Alamo Heights and Laurel Heights. In 1939, Olmos Park Estates (areas later added included Park Hills Estates, Olmos Park Terrace, Denver Park, Encino Estates, and Park Place) gained incorporation, when residents believed San Antonio mayor-to-be Maury Maverick would absorb the area into the city. As late as the mid-1940s, San Antonio Mayor Gus Mauerman, who despised Olmos Park, Terrell Hills, and Alamo Heights as "satellite cities" draining the San Antonio economy, tried unsuccessful legal action to have them unincorporated. Miller and Sanders write, "They became like so many Vaticans within Rome."

SCHERTZ
POPULATION: 18,694

This community, in far northeast Bexar County with a small portion in two adjoining counties, was settled in 1843 by Sebastian Schertz, after his family moved from Prince Solms' New Braunfels because of an unsettling relationship with the Native Americans. The settlement initially was called Cibolo (the Spanish word for "buffalo") Pit. It later took on the name Cut Off, because the community was cut off from civilization each time the Cibolo Creek flooded. The town was boosted by the arrival of the railroad in 1876 and renamed Schertz when William Schertz gave the railroad land for its depot. The town once again received a major boost with the opening of Randolph Air Force Base in 1930. Schertz was incorporated in 1958. Early Schertz was known in surrounding areas, including San Antonio, for the marksmanship of German immigrants. The town's annual shooting tournament was *Koenig Schiessen*, or King Shoot.

SELMA
POPULATION: 1,500

Even though this community in far northeast Bexar County was settled by Germans, the name "Selma" has no meaning in German. So, the origin of the town's name is not known. Most of the area was open cattle range up until 1870 when residents built a school, gristmill, cotton gin and post office. Selma officials are restoring the town's 1852 stage stop, which is a stop in an annual reenactment of the ride of the Pony Express along El Camino Real. A seventy-acre historical park is also being constructed along Cibolo Creek to tie into nearby Lookout Road, so named because a mount across an interstate loop in the City of San Antonio was a major lookout for the Comanches. Selma first incorporated in 1957, then unincorporated, then reincorporated in 1964.

SHAVANO PARK
POPULATION: 2,373

This town originally was part of the Stowers Ranch. Wallace Rogers & Sons purchased the land and developed it in far northwest Bexar County in 1948. The town incorporated in June 1956. Shavano is the Native American term for "mighty mountain."

SOMERSET
POPULATION: 1,550

This town in southwest Bexar County seems to be on wheels. In 1848, a group of Baptist families from Somerset, Kentucky, whose ancestors had come from Somerset, England, founded it in nearby Atascosa County. Next, the residents established a new townsite in Bexar three miles north around the turn of the nineteenth century and then moved to a new townsite nearby. The 1848 townsite took on the name of Old Somerset. While drilling for water at the new site, Carl Kurz, a town father, struck oil, and Somerset enjoyed an oil boom, the site of the largest known shallow field in the world at the time, serviced through two refineries and a pipeline to San Antonio. Lignite coal mining, cotton, fruit, corn production, and truck farming were added to the mix, but the Depression stagnated the town. Somerset was incorporated in 1973 as part of a plan to secure new utilities.

ST. HEDWIG
POPULATION: 1,875

This town in East Bexar County, with a land area second only to San Antonio in the county, was settled in the mid-nineteenth

An 1852 stagecoach stop is being restored with Texas Department of Transportation funds in the Bexar County suburban town of Selma.
COURTESY OF THE SELMA PARKS AND PRESERVATION COMMITTEE.

century by immigrants from the Polish region of Silesia. The town first was called Cottage Hill in the 1860s, but took on its present name in 1877, to honor Silesia's patron saint. St. Hedwig, largely a farming community, was incorporated in 1957 to prevent being absorbed by San Antonio, but had no officials for many years. Today, the town is in the process of building a new town hall.

TERRELL HILLS
POPULATION: 5,019

This town, incorporated in 1939 during a period when the City of San Antonio was attempting to expand, was formed from the farmlands of Dr. Frederick Terrell, a physician and banker who had been mayor pro tempore of San Antonio. Terrell's father had purchased the

Above: Carl Kurz and his children are outside their barn and stable in Somerset in south Bexar County in the 1890s.
COURTESY OF MARY LOU KLEMCKE AND THE INSTITUTE OF TEXAN CULTURES AT THE UNIVERSITY OF TEXAS AT SAN ANTONIO.

Below: The Somerset Oil Field in south Bexar County was a valuable resource in the 1920s.
COURTESY OF GEORGE PYRON SR. AND THE INSTITUTE OF TEXAN CULTURES AT THE UNIVERSITY OF TEXAS AT SAN ANTONIO.

land about 1880 when he was a general officer and paymaster at nearby Fort Sam Houston. Terrell Hills is one of the close-in "Tri Cities" and is a town made up of the residences of some of the most affluent citizens in the county. The town's city hall is a fire station built by San Antonio during the annexation fight.

UNIVERSAL CITY
POPULATION: 14,849

This town, in far northeast Bexar County, is the gateway to Randolph Air Force Base, opened in 1930. It has the largest wholly Bexar County population of any of the nine suburban cities in the metrocom area of three counties around the base. It was incorporated in 1960. There are two versions of how Universal City got its name: One, that it was named after a supply base for Universal Studios during the making of the film *West Point of the Air*, about Randolph; the other, that trainees came to Randolph from all around the world, or "universe," to live in a "universal city."

WINDCREST
POPULATION: 5,105

This town in northeast Bexar County is the result of a dream of Barbee and Murray Winn, who envisioned their cornfield becoming a city. The Winns, associated many years with the operation of the area's most-famous dime stores, Winn's, saw the dream become reality in September 1959, when fifty-one citizens incorporated Windcrest. The town is known widely as the "City of Lights," after a contest for Christmas house lighting sponsored each year by the Windcrest Women's Club. Travelers come from far and wide to see the lights of Windcrest each Yuletide.

Above: Blake Pyron in front of the Pyron Brothers Store in Somerset, c. 1924.
COURTESY OF GEORGE PYRON SR. AND THE INSTITUTE OF TEXAN CULTURES AT THE UNIVERSITY OF TEXAS AT SAN ANTONIO.

Below: The city hall and fire station for the suburban city of Terrell Hills was built as a fire station for San Antonio during a late 1930s annexation fight.

CHAPTER VII

THE RIVER: THE STREAM OF LIFE

Since the beginning of time, civilizations have risen or fallen on the basis of availability of water. Native Americans were attracted to the headwaters of the San Antonio River in Bexar County not only because there were buffalo, probably mastodons, alligators and deer, but mostly because there was an abundance of water. They believed the springs were sacred, as the water comes forth from Mother Earth as from a womb. The Native Americans first met Europeans at the site of water, and the Europeans located their facilities on existing waterways, such as the river and near San Pedro Springs and creek. Where there were no natural waterways, the Spanish built their own, as everyone needed water. They called these waterways *acequias*, or irrigation ditches. They had learned how to dig these ditches from the Arabs, and the word "acequia" is derived from Arabic, not Spanish. As early as 1723, huge ditches had been built. Some have said they were large enough to support canoe travel. However, considering the remaining *acequias* and their size and depth, it is very unlikely this is so. These ditches were engineering marvels, where water even flowed uphill, and one of the dams built (in the 1740s) at Mission Espada still is in use. Even though there probably were scores of the *acequias* built throughout the county, only minimal evidence of them exists. Most were filled in over the years, especially those at Concepción and San José. Each mission and the Villa de San Fernando had its dam and *acequia* system. There were more than fifty miles of *acequias*.

Water is intertwined in the history of Bexar and its existence in sufficient quantities is the reason for the continuing growth and development of the San Antonio River Valley. Today, most Bexar County residents receive water through their home faucets from an underground aquifer, but there is continual talk of ground water supplement needed.

Here are just a few of the highlights in the development of water-connected topics in Bexar:

- In 1718 an acequia separated the river and San Pedro Creek watersheds.
- In 1736 the first bridge to span the river was built, at today's Commerce Street, to allow foot traffic from the Alamo to cross the river. Santa Anna used this bridge to approach for the battle one hundred years later.
- In 1819 a major flood of the San Antonio River caused loss of lives and property.
- In 1830 the first regulations on the use of water from the river, creeks, and bridges were established since those of the Spanish in the eighteenth century.
- In 1858 the St. Mary's Street Bridge was built.
- In 1865 a major flood was followed by an outbreak of cholera. The first measures to minimize flooding were proposed, by controlling dams and construction along the river. In 1870, the city passed an ordinance to control river development.
- In 1899, following another major flood, an office of street cleaning and sanitation was developed, and the posts of two ditch commissioners were terminated.
- In 1900 the San Juan Ditch Company was founded to continue use of the oldest water right (1731) in Texas.
- In 1911, engineer W. E. Simpson proposed flood control by designing a conduit to divert and carry off storm water from the main channel of the river, rather than allowing it to flow through the river bend.
- In 1913 there was another major flood.
- In 1920-21 the firm of Metcalf and Eddy of Boston proposed constructing a flood retention dam in the Olmos Basin, just above the headwaters of the river, straightening the river channel and building a flood bypass channel through the downtown area.
- On September 21, 1921, a cloudburst dumped huge amounts of water over the basin and the river. Houston Street was nine feet deep in water. Fifty people were killed. Three years work

Opposite: The Blue Hole on the property of the University of the Incarnate Word in Olmos Basin is the spring which forms the headwaters of the San Antonio River.

Right: The Commerce Street bridge at the San Antonio River is shown about 1860. This is the bridge Santa Anna used to approach the Alamo.
COURTESY OF THE DAUGHTERS OF THE REPUBLIC OF TEXAS LIBRARY AT THE ALAMO.

Below: The Commerce Street bridge today.

on flood control began, including building Olmos Dam.
- In 1926 the flood bypass project was completed and Olmos Dam was completed the next year.
- On June 28, 1929, a visionary named Robert H. H. Hugman offered his "The Shops of Romula and Aragon," a plan to put gondolas on the river and to make significant river improvements to channel the flow and curb flooding. The early flurry of optimism over the plan gave way to the Depression, and everything stalled.
- In 1936, San Antonio River improvement was back in the news, when Jack White, the Plaza Hotel owner, and later, mayor, and the Mexican Businessmen's Association joined forces to stage the first river parade, "A Venetian Night," and the Texas Legislature created the San Antonio

River Authority as the controlling agent for the waterway.

- In 1938, White headed a committee to develop the river. On October 28, a special election was held and a .015 cents per $100 valuation tax was adopted to raise $75,000 to leverage $325,000 from the Works Progress Administration to fund river improvements. U.S. Representative Maury Maverick, later to be San Antonio's mayor, and Mayor C. K. Quin also were key leaders in getting the WPA plan into action. Beginning in October 1939, with Hugman as the chief river architect, work got underway with plans eventually to include a theater on the river (the Arneson) and the restoration of nearby La Villita under the direction of architect O'Neil Ford.
- At Fiesta, 1939, the city dedicated the river project and launched a new river parade two years later, under the auspices of the Texas

Above: The aftermath of the 1921 flood on Houston Street, the city's main street. The Gunter Hotel is on the left.

COURTESY OF CLARE BASS AND THE INSTITUTE OF TEXAN CULTURES AT THE UNIVERSITY OF TEXAS AT SAN ANTONIO.

Below: Olmos Dam in the Olmos Basin, shortly after its completion in 1927.

COURTESY OF THE SAN ANTONIO LIGHT COLLECTION, THE INSTITUTE OF TEXAN CULTURES AT THE UNIVERSITY OF TEXAS AT SAN ANTONIO.

Cavaliers, a men's civic, patriotic and social organization. The Cavaliers' King Antonio, refrigeration king George Friedrich, was the first Fiesta monarch to arrive in the city for Fiesta via boat, rather than via train or airplane. To mark changing times, the Cavaliers, originally an equestrian organization, placed a live horse on a river barge. Today, the Cavaliers continue the River Parade tradition and have re-established their horse patrol.

- The river project stood still during World War II, but events began to flow quite rapidly thereafter. Casa Rio became the first restaurant on the river walk in 1946 and

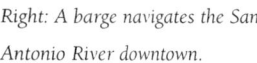

Right: A barge navigates the San Antonio River downtown.

Below: Mollie Bond Hayes christens a gondola on the San Antonio River in 1936 for an early-day river parade.
COURTESY OF THE SAN ANTONIO LIGHT COLLECTION,
THE INSTITUTE OF TEXAN CULTURES AT THE UNIVERSITY OF TEXAS AT SAN ANTONIO.

programs have run almost continually to improve the river not only downtown, but upstream to the northern edge of the business district and downstream past the missions under a river corridor plan. In 1959 a continual parade of new restaurants and hotels along the downtown river began, when another visionary, business-man David Straus, formed a tourist attraction committee under auspices of the Greater San Antonio Chamber of Commerce to spur commercial develop-ment of the river. The development included the approval of a $500,000 bond issue in 1964 to develop *Paseo del Rio*, the River Walk, which has become a tourist attraction to rival even the Alamo.

- In 1968, among the unique projects along the river was construction by San Antonio construction magnate H. B. Zachry, of the Hilton Palacio del Rio. This hotel, constructed to help meet room needs for the city's world's fair, was built as a shell and the

Above: The headquarters of the San Antonio Conservation Society in the King William District.

Below: Roger Hill, Jr., a recent Texas Cavaliers' King Antonio, meets his subjects from a barge during the Texas Cavaliers River Parade during Fiesta Week.
COURTESY OF PARISH PHOTOGRAPHY, INC.

Above: The San Antonio Turnverein entertained on Bowen's Island on the San Antonio River in the late 1800s.
COURTESY OF THE THE DAUGHTERS OF THE REPUBLIC OF TEXAS LIBRARY AT THE ALAMO, GRANDJEAN COLLECTION.

Right: Scholz Palm Garden, in the 100 block of Loyola Street on the San Antonio River, was a popular spot at the turn of the twentieth century.
COURTESY OF THE SAN ANTONIO CONSERVATION SOCIETY FOUNDATION, RABA COLLECTION.

Above: The construction of the Arneson River Theater on the San Antonio River Bend in the late 1930s as a Works Progress Administration project.
COURTESY OF THE *SAN ANTONIO LIGHT* COLLECTION, THE INSTITUTE OF TEXAN CULTURES AT THE UNIVERSITY OF TEXAS AT SAN ANTONIO.

Left: The Arneson River Theater today.

Above: U.S. Representative/San Antonio Mayor Maury Maverick (left) meets with President Franklin Roosevelt. Maverick was one of those responsible for the development of the San Antonio River downtown.

COURTESY OF THE SAN ANTONIO LIGHT COLLECTION, THE INSTITUTE OF TEXAN CULTURES AT THE UNIVERSITY OF TEXAS AT SAN ANTONIO.

Below: A low-water crossing in Brackenridge Park, c. 1920. Photo by Atlee B. Ayres.

COURTESY OF ANN RUSSELL AND THE SAN ANTONIO LIGHT COLLECTION, THE INSTITUTE OF TEXAN CULTURES AT THE UNIVERSITY OF TEXAS AT SAN ANTONIO.

rooms, completely furnished, were stacked into the shell, as if putting drawers into a chest. Throughout the river development, the river's bend, *Paseo del Rio*, has been extended, first into a lagoon of a new convention center, then into a second lagoon of the new Rivercenter Mall and Marriott Hotel. The city added attractions, including a holiday river parade during each Thanksgiving weekend, under the auspices of the river association.

- In 1987, in a more expansive program to divert floodwaters through the downtown area from the north, the city constructed a tunnel under the central business district. The construction took a decade. The tunnel met its first test, successfully, when another major flood hit the county

Left: Bexar County citizens at leisure at the San Pedro Park springs, c. 1880.

COURTESY OF THOMAS W. CUTRER AND THE INSTITUTE OF TEXAN CULTURES AT THE UNIVERSITY OF TEXAS AT SAN ANTONIO.

Below: Jack Sellers (left), Mrs. Jack Sellers, Mrs. Nada Schreur, and Willie Mae Johnson are on horseback in the San Antonio River in Brackenridge Park on August 30, 1938.

COURTESY OF THE SAN ANTONIO LIGHT COLLECTION, THE INSTITUTE OF TEXAN CULTURES AT THE UNIVERSITY OF TEXAS AT SAN ANTONIO.

in October 1998, and the floodwaters went underground.

- In November 1998 the county and city joined to form the San Antonio River Oversight Committee, to oversee the further development of the river as far south as Mission Espada. The Mission Trails project begins at the Alamo and ends at Espada. Besides river and street improvement, there will be hike and bike trails along the entire route, through historic neighborhoods such as King William.

Thus, the history of the area will come full circle. The Spaniards first encountered the native population in that same area more than three hundred years ago, and there is little doubt that the Native Americans, even without twenty-first century methods to control flooding, had been handling the river with care for centuries before.

Chapter VII ✦ 117

CHAPTER VIII

BEXAR COUNTY COMES OF AGE

Bexar County came out of World War II on a high note. The county's military installations had played a major role in training for the conflict. Returning GIs had high hopes of a better life. That better life began to blossom in the 1960s, as the county began an upward climb and worked on infrastructure improvements to support the community.

In the 1960s the county was running out of jail space. In 1962 the county opened a new state-of-the art jail on Laredo Street, near the police headquarters. Within a decade it was bursting at the seams with prisoner population, and the federal court ordered a new jail be built. The facility had a bed capacity of 750, and it was housing up to 1,500 prisoners. In 1988 a new jail—an Adult Detention Center of Bexar County—opened on Comal Street less than a mile to the west, while a third of the facility still was under construction. A shifting of prisoners from the overcrowded state prison system caused the 3,878-capacity jail to house up to 4,500, so the county opened an annex across the street in a warehouse area. In 2002 the county expanded the annex to house up to 1,429 prisoners.

There was a major western expansion of Interstate Highway 10 and the opening of the first section of Loop 1604, from Bandera Road to IH 10, in 1964. That same year the last Missouri-Kansas-Texas passenger train arrived in San Antonio. M-K-T lost its mail hauling contract to truckers, closed the depot, and demolished it four years later. In 1967, Loop 410, encircling San Antonio in 52 miles, opened, as did another major section of Loop 1604. On September 29, 1970, the last Missouri Pacific "Eagle" left San Antonio, without ceremony. In 1971, AMTRAK took over all passenger service in the nation, replacing Southern Pacific in San Antonio as the last independent carrier. AMTRAK took over the Southern Pacific Depot on East Commerce. From that point until 2000, rapid changes occurred in transportation facilities in the county—VIA Metropolitan Transit was formed, the last section of Loop 1604 was completed, Union Pacific took over Missouri Pacific and the San Antonio International Airport opened another terminal. Union Pacific took over M-K-T, then merged with Southern Pacific. This made all rail lines in the area under the control of Union Pacific, with Burlington Northern given some track rights, an element which came into play as plans were discussed to supply the new Toyota plant in southern Bexar County for its opening in 2006. AMTRAK could not maintain all the Southern Pacific Depot, so it leased it to an entertainment consortium, including the San Antonio international construction firm, Zachry Construction Corporation. It was renamed Sunset Station. AMTRAK still maintains a small facility at the depot but since January 1999 the 1902 structure primarily has been a restaurant and specialty retail center. More than $15 million has been invested into the redevelopment area around the depot, St. Paul Square, an attractive main street development between the Alamo and the Alamodome and East Bexar County. Positive support of that neighborhood has become a key element in the redevelopment of the area.

The predecessor of Zachry Construction Corporation was the H. B. Zachry Company, formed in Laredo in 1924 by the late H. B. "Pat" Zachry, who was a key leader in the development of the world's fair for San Antonio. The firm later moved to San Antonio. It is one of the world's largest construction and industrial maintenance service companies.

HemisFair '68 was one of the events that "made" Bexar County. This world's fair not only brought attention to Bexar County, but it also set the stage for so many positive things to come. The fair was an example of the "domino theory" in economic development for the county.

The fair opened April 6, 1968, at the eastern edge of downtown San Antonio on land which had been slated for urban renewal. Federal renewal funds could be used in the project, and historic structures (even though some were torn down, tragically) were restored. The city built a banquet-

Opposite: The San Antonio skyline in the mid-1990s. Photo by Roberta Barnes.

COURTESY OF THE SAN ANTONIO ECONOMIC DEVELOPMENT FOUNDATION.

Right: The Laredo Street Jail, September 1962.
COURTESY OF THE ZINTGRAFF COLLECTION, THE INSTITUTE OF TEXAN CULTURES AT THE UNIVERSITY OF TEXAS AT SAN ANTONIO AND THE BEXAR COUNTY SHERIFFS OFFICE.

Below: The Comal Street Jail in 2003.
COURTESY OF THE BEXAR COUNTY SHERIFFS OFFICE.

exhibit hall and arena, and the Tower of the Americas, for the fair. HemisFair was themed "The Confluence of Civilizations in the Americas." The fair ran for six months and enlisted the leadership talents of some of the major forces in the county. It left a legacy which changed both the physical nature of the area and launched the "can do" attitude of average citizens. The fair's U.S. Pavilion became the new federal courthouse, and the Texas pavilion became the Institute of Texan Cultures. The fairgrounds became a city park, HemisFair Park, with its water fountains and children's playground. In his book *HemisFair '68 and the Transformation of San Antonio*, Sterlin Holmesly outlines the legacy of the world's fair, including

Left: The Comal Street Jail Annex in 2003.
COURTESY OF THE BEXAR COUNTY SHERIFFS OFFICE.

Bottom, left: H. B. "Pat" Zachry, one of the founders of HemisFair, in 1979.
COURTESY OF THE SAN ANTONIO LIGHT COLLECTION, THE INSTITUTE OF TEXAN CULTURES AT THE UNIVERSITY OF TEXAS AT SAN ANTONIO.

Below: The construction of Zachry's Hilton Palacio del Rio Hotel, December 1967. Rooms were outfitted and lifted into place.
COURTESY OF JOHN AND DELA WHITE AND THE ZINTGRAFF COLLECTION, THE INSTITUTE OF TEXAN CULTURES AT THE UNIVERSITY OF TEXAS AT SAN ANTONIO.

a new municipal convention center, the facility which had been the exhibit hall, as the showplace of a revitalized tourist industry. He also chronicles the move of the ABA Dallas Chaparrals to San Antonio as the city's NBA franchise, the San Antonio Spurs. "HemisFair '68 proved to be a watershed event for San Antonio," Holmesly writes, "one that unified and changed the city. Its legacy is still changing the city." The term "HemisFair" was coined by a leading businessman, Jerome Harris. Political leaders such as U.S. Representative Henry Gonzalez, Texas Governor John Connally, and San Antonio Mayor Walter McAllister worked alongside business leaders such as Zachry, Bill Sinkin, and B. J. "Red" McCombs.

Newcomer retired Brigadier General Robert McDermott, who had begun to shepherd the gigantic United Services Automobile Association (USAA), an insurance empire, drew a vision for growth from the fair. As president of the Greater San Antonio Chamber of Commerce, he founded the Economic Development Foundation, which has been responsible for attracting tens of

Chapter VIII ♦ 121

Above: President and Mrs. Lyndon Johnson visit the U.S. Pavilion at HemisFair in July 1968.

COURTESY OF JOHN AND DELA WHITE AND THE ZINTGRAFF COLLECTION, THE INSTITUTE OF TEXAN CULTURES AT THE UNIVERSITY OF TEXAS AT SAN ANTONIO.

Right: Businessman Jerome K. Harris (left), who coined the term "HemisFair," with young people at the fair, July 1968.

COURTESY OF THE SAN ANTONIO LIGHT COLLECTION, THE INSTITUTE OF TEXAN CULTURES AT THE UNIVERSITY OF TEXAS AT SAN ANTONIO.

thousands of jobs to the city, as well as major corporations such as SBC and Toyota. SBC moved from St. Louis to San Antonio. McDermott's USAA had been established in 1922 by a group of twenty-five Army officers who had difficulty obtaining reliable automobile insurance coverage because they were considered transient and bad risks. Today, USAA, headquartered in

Left: USAA (United Services Automobile Association) headquarters in northwest Bexar County. The firm is one of the county's major employers.
COURTESY OF USAA.

Below: The Tower of the Americas was the theme structure for HemisFair.
COURTESY OF JOHN AND DELA WHITE AND THE ZINTGRAFF COLLECTION, THE INSTITUTE OF TEXAN CULTURES AT THE UNIVERSITY OF TEXAS AT SAN ANTONIO.

San Antonio with other major office locations in Arizona, Virginia, Colorado, Florida, California, and Germany and with twenty-two thousand employees, is one of the largest property/casualty insurers in the United States.

The positive attitude which was at the basis of the fair laid the groundwork for other political and civic work of people such as Mayors Lila Cockrell and Henry Cisneros and County Judge Cyndi Taylor Krier. Cisneros often is addressed as the first Hispanic *alcalde* of San Antonio in modern times, even though there certainly were scores of Hispanic mayors in the Spanish colonial period. Krier, a former state senator, served from 1992-2001 as the county's first female county judge. Historically, the Bexar County Courthouse has been Democratic, with San Antonio a stronghold for that party. In the latter part of the twentieth century, the GOP made major inroads, especially in electing various levels of judges in the county system.

Nelson Wolff, a Democrat who succeeded Krier as Bexar County's forty-second county justice/judge in 2001, is one of three men to have been both mayor and county judge, Samuel Maverick and Bryan Callaghan being the other two. Wolff also was a state legislator and senator. As county judge, he has proven himself a champion of county-city cooperation. He has proposed bond elections, joint tax phasing agreements and programs to unify paperwork in the justice system. The city's sixty-five-hundred-capacity baseball stadium, home of the San Antonio Missions, is named for him. His wife, Tracy Wolff, is founder and president of the Hidalgo Foundation of Bexar County. It was formed in 2001 to raise $6 million in public funds

Right: Judge John Specia (left) is with Tracy Wolff, John L. Nau III, chairman of the Texas Historical Commission, and County Judge Nelson Wolff at the re-dedication of the Bexar County Courthouse in April 2003.

Below: The Nelson Wolff Municipal Stadium, home of the San Antonio Missions, is named for the current county judge and former mayor. He is one of three men to have served in both capacities.

toward the $23 million restoration of the Bexar County Courthouse. State and county funds are also part of the restoration, which includes returning some courtrooms to their ambience of the 1920s, but with 2004 technology. Plans include housing the state's first comprehensive children's court.

The courthouse shares Plaza de las Islas with San Fernando Cathedral and other such structures as the just-renovated Bell Building, which was the headquarters for Santa Anna during the Battle of the Alamo. One can walk around the plaza and read at least a half dozen plaques outlining important events that have happened there. Through the years, county justices/judges were appointed variously by the governor, the congress or president of the Republic or the Union authorities, or elected. Charles Anderson served the longest as the county judge, from January 1, 1939, to August 14, 1964, though Al M. Heck filled in for him while he was on active military duty.

Between the late 1920s and the mid-1960s, there were no major changes in the courthouse. Architect Edward R. Gondeck conducted interior remodeling in 1963 and a $2.6 million remodeling and modernization in 1970, a project which some consider not compatible with the 1897 building. A sixth floor over part of the courthouse was added in 1973 and major exterior cleanups were completed in the early 1980s and in 1993.

Top: The Bexar County Courthouse in 2003.

Middle: The controversial "Gondeck Addition" on the west side of the Bexar County Courthouse. Critics say it does not fit the design of the 1890s building.

Bottom: The Cadena-Reeves Justice Center on the west side of the courthouse is named for two late distinguished Bexar County jurists.

Right: The Southern Pacific Railroad Station on East Commerce, c. 1926.
COURTESY OF THE INSTITUTE OF TEXAN CULTURES AT THE UNIVERSITY OF TEXAS AT SAN ANTONIO.

Below: The Southern Pacific Railroad Station in 2003, after its renovation.

The old red courthouse has seen many "firsts" through the years: County Judge Robert B. Green was a district judge in his twenties, believed to hold the record as the youngest man ever to serve such a high court. In 1964, E. F. "Hippo" Garcia became the first Mexican-American judge of a local county court of record. He later became the first Mexican American to serve locally as a federal judge. In the early 1970s, John Benavides became the first local Mexican American district judge. In 1977, Carol Haberman became the first woman elected to a Bexar district court. In 1992, Rose Spector, a Bexar County district judge, became the first woman elected to the Texas Supreme Court.

As early as 1977, discussions began on extending county court facilities across Main Avenue to the west, and ground was broken in 1988 for the Bexar County Justice Center, now named the Cadena-Reeves Justice Center, after two noted Bexar County jurists, Carlos Cadena and Blair "Bruzzy" Reeves. Reeves, as county

judge, had marshaled the legislature support to create a tax to finish construction of the county's teaching hospital, laying the groundwork for the University of Texas Health Science Center at San Antonio, the cornerstone for the South Texas Medical Center. This vote by county leaders was another of the watershed developments of 1968.

The medical center, another example of "clump" development in the county, is a seven-hundred-acre medical complex in northwest Bexar, composed not only of the state medical, dental, and nursing schools, but also of 18 other institutions, including six major hospitals. Development of the county's medical area began as early as 1944, with the San Antonio Medical Foundation created in 1947. Before major development began, there was a controversy over whether the center would be housed in downtown San Antonio or at its current site, in the Oak Hills area. The Southwest Texas Methodist Hospital had been located earlier at the site. The center now has a plant and equipment value of $1.7 billion, employment of nearly 30,000 people, more than 100,000 inpatients and 3.6 million outpatients each year. During the county judgeship of Reeves, the county commissioners in December 1971 adopted the official Bexar County coat-of-arms.

Partly because of the expertise brought by the medical center and partly because of the genius and vision of such men as the late Tom Slick, Jr., and McDermott (Texas Research and Technology Foundation and Texas Research Park), Bexar County has gained a reputation for the development of biotechnology.

In December 1941, Slick, an inventor, oilman, rancher, engineer, philanthropist, peacemaker, and adventurer, established the Foundation of Applied Research at his Essar (the phonetic spelling of "S.R.," for scientific research) Ranch in west Bexar. It now is the Southwest Foundation for Biomedical Research. SFBR has five research departments—

Above: Blair "Bruzzy" Reeves was the county judge who set up the mechanics for the development of the South Texas Medical Center.

COURTESY OF THE SAN ANTONIO LIGHT COLLECTION, THE INSTITUTE OF TEXAN CULTURES AT THE UNIVERSITY OF TEXAS AT SAN ANTONIO.

Below: The site of a dairy in northwest Bexar County in the 1940s now is the hub of the South Texas Medical Center.

COURTESY OF THE UNIVERSITY OF TEXAS HEALTH SCIENCE CENTER AT SAN ANTONIO AND THE SAN ANTONIO MEDICAL FOUNDATION.

Right: The South Texas Medical Center in northwest Bexar County.
COURTESY OF THE UNIVERSITY OF TEXAS HEALTH SCIENCE CENTER AT SAN ANTONIO AND THE SAN ANTONIO MEDICAL FOUNDATION.

Below: A locator map of the South Texas Medical Center in 2000.
COURTESY OF JIM REED, THE SAN ANTONIO MEDICAL FOUNDATION.

Opposite, top: Harold Vagtborg (left), first president of the Southwest Research Institute in west Bexar County, talks with Tom Slick, Jr., the founder of SwRI®.
COURTESY OF THE SOUTHWEST RESEARCH INSTITUTE COMMUNICATIONS DEPARTMENT.

Opposite, bottom: Tom Slick, Jr., and the board of the Southwest Research Institute.
COURTESY OF THE SOUTHWEST RESEARCH INSTITUTE COMMUNICATIONS DEPARTMENT.

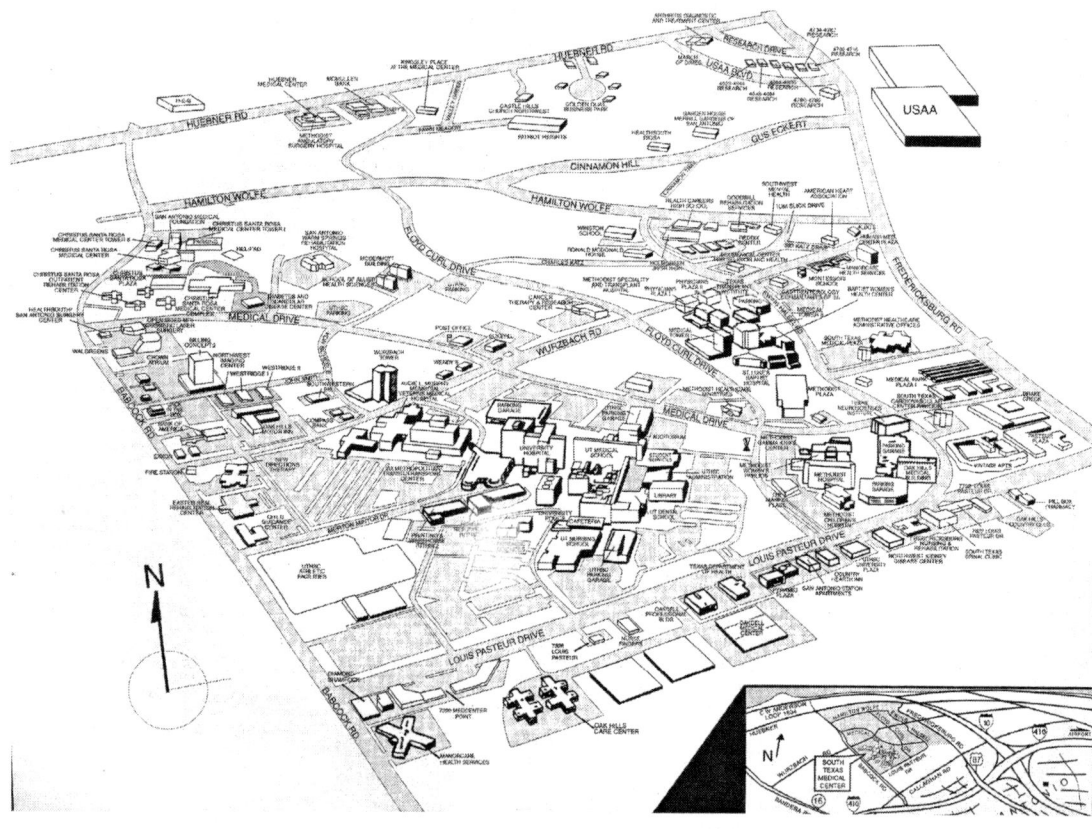

genetics; physiology and medicine; virology and immunology; organic chemistry; and comparative medicine—and, with its 70 doctoral-level scientists among its workforce of 370, has produced 180 research projects addressing AIDS, cancer, diabetes, heart disease, hepatitis, herpes, malaria, and other parasitic infections, osteoporosis, premature lung disease, and psychiatric disorders. The foundation has a 332-acre campus in west Bexar and includes the Southwest National Primate Research Center, one of only eight such centers in the United States and the only one in the Southwest. It is the home of the world's largest colony of baboons for biomedical research.

In 1947, Slick founded Southwest Research Institute as a civilian high-tech facility. Today, it has grown into an internationally known applied engineering and physical sciences research and development organization, with twenty-eight hundred employees and almost two million square feet of laboratory, workshop, and office space in west Bexar. SwRI® has ties to the nation's new homeland security sector. When Louis Pasteur said that "laboratories for scientific research are sacred places where the future is born," he must have had a look into the future of such facilities as those founded by Slick. The development of the Texas Research Park, still being filled in far southwest Bexar County, might be another major technology success story.

While the county was enjoying new life in the creation of biotechnical facilities, the literary life of the community was not being ignored. In the early 1990s, an old Sears store was demolished on Romana Plaza and the space went to a new Central Library, designed by famed Mexican architect Ricardo Legorreta. In 2003 the library system celebrated its centennial.

Another area of business which took on new flavor was Bolner's Fiesta Products, which promotes itself as the Tower of Babel of spices. Since 1955 the family-owned San Antonio business has been importing spices from all over the world and produces its own Mexican spices in its Bexar County headquarters.

Development of major shopping malls began in the county in the early 1960s and continues today. Earlier malls were (and continue to be) under one roof, while newer malls such as the Alamo Quarry and The Forum are composed of many freestanding buildings.

The emboldened attitude which came with HemisFair had wide effects on the community, encouraging political activism against the background of the 1960s, the Federal Model Cities Project and labor organizer Saul Alinsky. Two community action organizations, Communities Organized for Public Service (COPS), energized by its affiliation to the Catholic Church, and Metro Alliance, also with religious affiliation, came into being.

The Southwest Foundation for Biomedical Research in west Bexar County houses, among many scientific entities, the largest baboon colony for biomedical research in the Southwest.
COURTESY OF THE SOUTHWEST FOUNDATION FOR BIOMEDICAL RESEARCH.

While HemisFair underlined the value of the tourist trade in Bexar County, tourism long has been a nongovernmental provider of jobs in the area. The San Antonio Zoo is one of the oldest in the nation. As early as 1870, poet and author Sidney Lanier described caged animal exhibits in San Pedro Park, including a Mexican lion, a bear pit, a wolf, a coyote, and an aviary. In 1912, George Brackenridge fenced an area in what is now the Brackenridge Golf Course and housed ten buffalo and six elk from Yellowstone National Park, a number of deer, cages of monkeys, a pair of lions and four bears. In 1914 he moved the animals north to what now is the zoo. Two years later, the city officially designated the area as the zoo, after Brackenridge gave the land, an original Spanish land grant, to the city.

Above: The Main Library, an adaptive re-use on the site of a former Sears store, is known as the "red enchilada."
COURTESY OF THE SAN ANTONIO PUBLIC LIBRARY

Below: George Brackenridge had buffalo in the zoo which was the predecessor to the San Antonio Zoo. Here, a bison greets visitors to the zoo in 1939.
COURTESY OF THE SAN ANTONIO LIGHT COLLECTION, THE INSTITUTE OF TEXAN CULTURES AT THE UNIVERSITY OF TEXAS AT SAN ANTONIO.

Right: Arthur Geissler, director of the Texas Theater Orchestra, charms bears at the San Antonio Zoo with his violin playing in February 1927.
COURTESY OF THE SAN ANTONIO LIGHT COLLECTION, THE INSTITUTE OF TEXAN CULTURES AT THE UNIVERSITY OF TEXAS AT SAN ANTONIO.

Below: The hippos at the San Antonio Zoo have been a perennial favorite. This hippopotamus arrived at the zoo on October 5, 1931.
COURTESY OF THE SAN ANTONIO LIGHT COLLECTION, THE INSTITUTE OF TEXAN CULTURES AT THE UNIVERSITY OF TEXAS AT SAN ANTONIO.

Diversification in the county's tourist trade came in the latter years of the twentieth century, with the opening of Sea World San Antonio and Fiesta Texas, the latter by USAA and Opryland (later sold to Six Flags) both in the far western area of the county. Retama Park, a horse racing track in Selma on the northern edge of the county, also attracts some visitors. The latter was made possible after pari-mutuel racing in Texas was legalized in 1987, after a fifty-year absence. Alamo Downs on the west side of the county was closed in the late 1930s by a Texas governor opposed to horse betting. Among the newest of the county's tourist attractions is the twenty-thousand-seat Verizon Wireless Amphitheater, in Selma, that has held numerous popular concerts. All these facilities bring millions of tourists to San Antonio each year.

Perhaps the most-successful business entertainment venture in Bexar County in the twentieth century was the creation of the San Antonio Spurs. The former ABA Dallas Chaparrals team was moved to the Alamo City in 1973 by twenty-seven visionary businessmen who never could have dreamed what effect the team would have on the area. In June 2003 the Spurs celebrated their second NBA championship and have brought San Antonio to the attention of potential tourists. The first home of the Spurs was the HemisFair Arena. In 1993, the city opened the Alamodome, with its roof spanning nine acres, as a major sixty-five-thousand-seat multi-purpose, entertainment and convention facility. The Spurs decided to play in the Dome later. The $186-million project was funded through a special sales tax.

In November 1999, Bexar County voters approved a County-led partnership among the Spurs, Bexar County, the San Antonio Stock Show and Rodeo and the Coliseum Advisory Board to build a $175-million community facility. It is adjacent to the Freeman Coliseum and serves as the current home for the Spurs and the San Antonio Livestock Exposition. SBC was the naming partner. The Spurs contributed $28.5 million and the county $146.5 million, and the SBC Center opened in October 2002. The center provides 18,797 regular seats including 1,800 charter seats and special suites for Spurs games.

Minor league baseball has been a staple in Bexar County for more than one hundred years. Today, that love of the sport is centered in the San Antonio Missions Baseball Club. The club was established in 1888 as a charter member of the Texas League. The team has been affiliated with such major league organizations as the St. Louis Browns (1933-42 and 1946-53), Baltimore Orioles (1954-58), Chicago Cubs (1959-62 and 1968-71), Houston Colt 45s/Astros (1963-64), Milwaukee Brewers (1972), Cleveland Indians (1973-75), Texas Rangers (1976), Los Angeles Dodgers (1977-2000), and the Seattle Mariners (2001-present). The Missions have won ten Texas League championship titles and back-to-back Texas League championships in 2002 and

Six Flags Fiesta Texas was one of the theme parks which opened in Bexar County in the latter part of the twentieth century.
COURTESY OF FIESTA TEXAS.

Right: Alamo Downs in west Bexar County was a favorite for horse racing fans in the early part of the twentieth century. It was closed by the Texas governor in the 1930s.
COURTESY OF THE SAN ANTONIO LIGHT COLLECTION, THE INSTITUTE OF TEXAN CULTURES AT THE UNIVERSITY OF TEXAS AT SAN ANTONIO.

Below: Retama Park in north Bexar County brought pari-mutuel betting back to Bexar County in the 1990s. The track is located in Selma.
COURTESY OF JOE STRAUS.

Above: Sea World is a theme park bringing revenue to the Bexar County economy.
COURTESY OF SEA WORLD.

Left: The Alamodome, now a decade old, soon will undergo renovation. Photo by Kurt Ghelhaar.
COURTESY OF FOTOGRAFIKA

Chapter VIII ♦ 135

Above: The SBC Center opened in October 2002 as the new home of the Spurs and the San Antonio Stock Show and Rodeo.
COURTESY OF SBC COMMUNICATIONS, INC.

Below: Tim Duncan (left) and David Robinson have been leading Bexar County citizens as members of the NBA champs, the Spurs.
COURTESY OF THE SPURS, THE NATIONAL BASKETBALL ASSOCIATION, AND SBC COMMUNICATIONS, INC.

2003. The Missions have had four Hall of Famers come through their organization over the years. They are Joe Morgan, Billy Williams, Brooks Robinson, and Dennis Eckersley. Recent stars who have stopped in San Antonio on their way to the big leagues include Pedro Martinez, Fernando de Valenzuela, Mike Piazza, Orel Hershiser, and Eric Gagne (the 2003 National League Cy Young Award winner). In 2003, the Missions' manager, Dave Brundage, was named "Minor League Manager of the Year." This is the first time in the history of the Missions that such an honor has been awarded to the manager. The Missions' stadium, the Nelson W. Wolff Municipal Baseball Stadium, opened in April 1994. It has a multi-purpose design that allows for events such as professional baseball, concerts, boxing and high school, college and amateur sports.

In 2006 the $800-million Toyota Motor Corporation plant will open in south Bexar County, employing two thousand workers to produce Toyota's big truck, the Tundra. Toyota, an environmentally friendly company, purchased three thousand acres for the plant and has pledged to retain buildings of a Spanish land grant ranch as well as parklands along the Medina River.

Ironically, county leaders tried for years to develop the county's south side, including a defeated drive to locate the University of Texas at San Antonio there. Now, a Japanese auto manufacturer has taken action. Also ironically, development in south Bexar was stifled for years because of the existence of Mitchell Lake, a city sewage lake. The new Toyota plant is adjacent to a recycling plant (a fancier name for a sewer plant) and just down the road from the lake and a city golf course, expensive homes, and the city's police academy. San Antonio Mayor Ed Garza has made the Toyota area a main plank in his South Side Business Initiative, with suppliers making plans to build facilities adjacent to the Toyota site.

The interdependency of the elements of history also is shown in the Mitchell Lake area. The lake has become a wildlife refuge under the sponsorship of the San Antonio Water System, the San Antonio Audobon Society, and the Mitchell Lake Wetlands Society. The new headquarters for the Mitchell Lake Wetlands

Above: The backwaters of Mitchell Lake bring wildlife to south Bexar County.

Left: The Mitchell Lake Wetlands Society has moved the John Palmer Leeper house to a location in south Bexar County for use as the society's headquarters.

Below: Cattle ranching continues a part of the economy of the Hill Country near Bexar County.

COURTESY OF JOHN AND DELA WHITE AND THE ZINTGRAFF COLLECTION, THE INSTITUTE OF TEXAN CULTURES AT THE UNIVERSITY OF TEXAS AT SAN ANTONIO.

138 ✦ HISTORIC BEXAR COUNTY

Society is an historic home, the Leeper House, moved from the grounds of the McNay Art Museum. The house was the dwelling of Marion Koogler McNay while she was building her Sunset Hills mansion in north Bexar. The structure later was the home of John Palmer Leeper, long-time McNay director.

Today one can stand at the edge of the Olmos Basin, where all this development began more than ten thousand years ago, squint one's eyes and see the progression of civilization through the San Antonio River Valley. There are the Native Americans, traveling perhaps to the site of the Toyota plant, the Spaniards entering the

Opposite, top: Signs mark the coming of the Toyota truck plant to south Bexar County.

Opposite, bottom: A glimpse into the economic future of south Bexar County is shown in this photo on construction of a Tundra truck at Toyota's Kentucky plant.
COURTESY OF TOYOTA MOTOR COMPANY

Above: Earl Abel's, a Broadway Street restaurant just south of Alamo Heights, has been a favorite eating spot for seventy years.
COURTESY OF JOHN AND DELA WHITE AND THE ZINTGRAFF COLLECTION, THE INSTITUTE OF TEXAN CULTURES AT THE UNIVERSITY OF TEXAS AT SAN ANTONIO.

Left: One Hispanic influence on San Antonio is seen in this Charreada at the San Antonio Charro Ranch in May 1989.
COURTESY OF THE SAN ANTONIO EXPRESS-NEWS COLLECTION, THE INSTITUTE OF TEXAN CULTURES AT THE UNIVERSITY OF TEXAS AT SAN ANTONIO.

Chapter VIII ♦ 139

Above: The St. Paul Square area on the city's near East Side is shown in 1917.
COURTESY OF STANLEY H. SCHMIDT AND THE INSTITUTE OF TEXAN CULTURES AT THE UNIVERSITY OF TEXAS AT SAN ANTONIO.

Right: St. Paul Square in 2003, after renovation.

Left: Frost National Bank.
Courtesy of Frost National Bank.

Below: The HemisFair grounds became a city park after the close of the fair.

Chapter VIII ◆ 141

Above: El Mercado, the Mexican market in downtown San Antonio, is a favorite spot for locals and tourists alike.

Below: This cement plant site, shown in 1926, now is a busy shopping mall, the Quarry Market.

area, the Anglo-American and European settlers arriving, the *tejanos* contemplating their future and the many faces of newer immigrants seeking a new home. As some in the Northeast might date themselves from their American Revolution ancestors, so citizens of Bexar County often find their identity—their roots—in connections to those of the Spanish colonial period, the Texas Revolution or immigrants from the mid-1800s. If this work has done nothing more than tweak the curiosity of citizens to find out more about how their forebears changed Bexar County—for better or for worse—the goals of this narrative have been achieved.

The story ends as it began, in the Olmos Basin. The Native Americans of ten thousand years ago would have marveled at the dam that now dominates the landscape.

Chapter VIII ♦ 143

RESOURCES

Material for this work came from interviews and discussions with Bexar County historians and citizen historians, attendance at conferences and seminars targeting Bexar County history, the author's personal knowledge of Bexar County history and research in many types of publications. Following are some of the major sources used. No attempt has been made to cite essays solicited by the author from companies, schools, school districts and suburban cities. Also, no attempt has been made to cite Web sites addressing the same types of topics.

Almaraz, Felix D., Jr. *Governor Antonio Martinez and Mexican Independence in Texas: An Orderly Transition.* San Antonio: Bexar County Historical Commission, 1997, reprinted with the permission of *The Permian Historical Annual*, Volume 15, December 1975.

Almaraz, Felix D., Jr. "San Antonio Missions After Secularization, 1800-1883," manuscript, 1984.

Almaraz, Felix D., Jr. *The San Antonio Missions and Their System of Land Tenure.* Austin: The University of Texas Press, 1989.

Almaraz, Felix D., Jr. *Tragic Cavalier: Governor Manuel Saucedo of Texas, 1808-1813.* College Station: Texas A&M University Press, 1971.

Bowser, David. "San Antonio's Old Red-Light District: A History, 1890-1941," manuscript.

Buchanan, Sally. "Buchanan's Handy-Dandy Timeline of San Antonio (Mostly) River History," manuscript, 2003.

Carver Community Cultural Center and The University of Texas Institute of Texan Cultures. *The Houston Rio and Courts-Martial of 1917.* San Antonio: Carver Community Cultural Center, San Antonio, Texas, and The University of Texas Institute of Texan Cultures.

Casteneda, Carlos E., Ph.D. "The Mission Era: The Finding of Texas, 1519-1693," Volume 1, *Our Catholic Heritage in Texas, 1519-1936.* Austin: Von Boeckmann-Jones Company, 1936.

Chabot, Frederick C. *San Antonio and Its Beginnings, 1691-1731.* San Antonio: The Naylor Printing Company, 1931.

Chipman, Donald E. *Spanish Texas, 1519-1821.* Austin: University of Texas Press, 1992.

Clack, Cary. "The Legacy of the Carver." *San Antonio Express-News*, July 5, 2003.

Curtis, Albert. *Fabulous San Antonio.* San Antonio: The Naylor Printing Company, 1955.

Davis, John L. *Texans One and All.* San Antonio: The Institute of Texan Cultures, 1998.

Evett, Alice. "Fatal Corner." *San Antonio Monthly*, July 1992.

Fehrenbach, T. R. "Alamo Heights in Perspective." *Golden Anniversary Alamo Heights.* Alamo Heights: City of Alamo Heights, 1972.

Fisher, Lewis F. *C. H. Guenter & Son at 150 Years: The Legacy of a Texas Milling Pioneer.* San Antonio: Maverick Publishing Company, 2001.

Fisher, Lewis F. *Saving San Antonio: The Precarious Preservation of a Heritage.* Lubbock: Texas Tech University Press, 1996.

Fisher, Lewis F. *Balcones Heights: A Crossroads of San Antonio.* San Antonio: Maverick Publishing Company, 1999.

Fort Sam Houston Museum. *A Pocket Guide to Historic Fort Sam Houston.* Fort Sam Houston: Fort Sam Houston Museum, 2000.

Fort Sam Houston Museum. *Surrounded by History: How Fort Sam Houston Built Environment Embodies the Values of Distinguished Soldiers.* Fort Sam Houston: Fort Sam Houston Museum, 1999.

Fort Sam Houston Museum. *The Post at San Antonio, 1845-1879.* Fort Sam Houston: Fort Sam Houston Museum, 2002.

Frazier, Donald. "Texas Cowboys Riding the Trails." *Heritage Magazine*, Spring 2003.

Grabowska, John. *Gente de Razón* (film guide). National Park Service.

Green, David P. *Place Names of San Antonio.* San Antonio: Maverick Publishing Company, 2002.

Guerra, Henry. *San Antonio: A Unique History and Pictorial Guide.* San Antonio: The Alamo Press, 1998.

Guerra, Mary Ann Noonan. *The Missions of San Antonio.* San Antonio: The Alamo Press, 1982.

Guerra, Mary Ann Noonan. *The San Antonio River.* San Antonio: The Alamo Press, 1987.

Gussen, Mary Lee. *And the Snake Slept.*

Habig, Marion A., O.F.M., *The Alamo Chain of Missions: A History of San Antonio's Five Old Missions.* Revised Edition. Chicago: Franciscan Herald Press, 1968; reprinted by Pioneer Enterprises, 1997.

"The Handbook of Texas Online: Bexar County," 2003, The Texas State Historical Commission, http://www.tsha.utexas.edu/handbook/online.

The New Handbook of Texas in Six Volumes. Austin: The Texas State Historical Commission, 1996.

Haynes, David. *Character Endures: The Genealogy of Thomas Claiborne Frost.* San Antonio: Thomas Claiborne Frost IV, 2002.

Hendricks, Frances Kellam. *A History of Southwest Texas Methodist Hospital, 1955-1980.* San Antonio: Southwest Texas Methodist Hospital, 1983.

Holmesly, Sterlin. *HemisFair '68 and the Transformation of San Antonio.* San Antonio: Maverick Publishing Company, 2003.

Hunter, J. Marvin. *The Old Trail Drivers of Texas*. Revised 1985, Austin: The University of Texas Press; originally published under the direction of George W. Saunders, president of the Old Trail Drivers' Association, 1924.

Jackson, Jack. *Los Mesteños: Spanish Ranching in Texas, 1721-1821*. Texas A&M University Press, College Station, Texas, 1986.

Jennings, Frank W. *San Antonio: The Story of an Enchanted City*. Second Edition. Austin, Texas: Eakin Press, 2002.

Lam, May and Evelyn Crow. "The History of the Asian Community in San Antonio," 2003, manuscript

Lanzone, John A. *Horse, Next to Woman, God's Greatest Gift to Man: A History of the Straus-Frank Company*. San Antonio: The Straus-Frank Company, 1970.

Leeper, John Palmer, and Caroline Shelton. *Festivals of San Antonio*. San Antonio: Trinity University Press, 1983.

Matthews, Wilbur L. *History of the San Antonio Medical Foundation and the South Texas Medical Center*. Revised Edition. San Antonio Medical Foundation, 1988.

Matthews, Wilbur L. *History of the San Antonio Zoo*. San Antonio: San Antonio Zoological Society, 1990.

Miller, Char, and Heywood T. Sanders, "Olmos Park and the Creation of a Suburban Bastion, 1927-1939." *Urban Texas*. College Station: Texas A&M University Press, 1990.

Nasatir, Abraham P. *Borderland in Retreat: From Spanish Louisiana to the Far Southwest*. Albuquerque: University of New Mexico Press, 1976.

Office of History, HQ Twelfth Flying Training Wing. *A Brief History of Randolph AFB and the Twelfth Flying Wing*. Randolph Air Force Base, Texas, 2000.

Olmestead, Frederick Law. *A Journey Through Texas*. Austin: University of Texas Press.

Pfeiffer, Maria Watson. *School by the River: Ursuline Academy to Southwest School of Art, 1851-2001*. San Antonio: Maverick Publishing Company, 2001.

Russell, Jan Jarboe and Mark Langford. *San Antonio: A Cultural Tapestry*. Memphis: Towery Publishing Company, sponsored by The Greater San Antonio Chamber of Commerce, 1998.

A History of Military Aviation in San Antonio. San Antonio: U.S. Government Printing Office, 2000.

Santos, Sylvia Ann, Courthouses of Bexar County, 1731-1978, San Antonio: Bexar County Historical Commission, 1979.

Sexton, Kathryn and Irwin Sexton. *Samuel A. Maverick*. San Antonio: The Naylor Company, 1964.

Slattery, Sister Margaret Patrice, C.C.V.I. *Promises to Keep: Incarnate Word College: Glory for God, Unity for Others, Trouble for Ourselves*. San Antonio: The University of the Incarnate Word, 1995.

Texas Almanac, 2002-2003. Dallas: *Dallas Morning News*, distributed by the Texas A&M University Consortium, College Station, Texas, 2001.

The Texas Monthly Guidebook. Austin: Texas Monthly Press, Inc., 1982.

Thonhoff, Robert H. "The Vital Contribution of Texas in the Winning of the American Revolution." An essay. Karnes City: 2000, revised 2002.

3D International. *Bexar County Courthouse Historic Preservation Master Plan*. San Antonio, 2000.

Weller, Clara. *My Town, Kirby*. San Antonio: J&M Printing, Inc., 1989.

Walker, Tom. *Banking on Tradition: The 130-Year History of the Frost National Bank*. San Antonio: Frost National Bank, 2000.

Winders, Richard Bruce. *Sacrificed at the Alamo: Tragedy and Triumph in the Texas Revolution*. Abilene: State House Press, McMurry University, 2004.

Woolford, Sam. *San Antonio: A History for Tomorrow*. San Antonio: The Naylor Printing Company, 1963; published originally as a series in the *San Antonio Light*.

APPENDIX I

BEXAR COUNTY JUSTICES AND JUDGES

The following people, as reflected in a compilation from the Bexar County Archives, have served as either chief justices or county judges of Bexar County since the formation of the county. County judges were called chief justices until August 1866. Any gaps in the office of top county official are due to short periods when there were upheavals and various changes. At those times, officials may have been appointed or elected on a temporary basis. Those short-term periods are not addressed here. Bexar County was organized July 3, 1837, after an act of the Congress of the Republic of Texas on December 22, 1836.

CHIEF JUSTICES

Joseph Baker
Nominated by Sam Houston and confirmed by the Texas Senate, December 20, 1836. Served from July 3, 1837, when the county was organized, through the latter part of 1837.

Erasmo Seguin
Named by the president of the Republic of Texas, after the Texas Congress elected William A. H. Daingerfield and the president refused to commission him. Served from December 18, 1837, to January 9, 1840.

John H. Simpson
Elected and served from January 30, 1840, to July 14, 1842.

John McMullen
Named by the Texas Congress and served from December 9, 1842 to January 1, 1844.

David Morgan
Elected January 1, 1844 and served from April 1, 1844, to July 6, 1846.

Thomas Whitehead
Served from August 4, 1846 to February 17, 1848.

Ira L. Hewitt
Elected August 7, 1848 and served from August 29, 1848, to June 19, 1849.

John D. McLeod
Elected August 5, 1850, and August 2, 1852, 1855, and 1856, and served from August 19, 1849 to July 11, 1857.

William F. Weeks
Elected and served from August 27, 1857, to August 18, 1858.

John H. Duncan
Elected August 2, 1858 and August 6, 1860 and served from August 30, 1858 to July 22, 1862.

Peter Gallagher
Elected August 4, 1862 and served from August 18, 1862 until his resignation in 1863.

Samuel A. Maverick
Elected October 15, 1863 and 1864 and served from October 15, 1863 to June 10, 1865.

Augustus Siemering
Appointed and served from August 12, 1865 to August 18, 1866.

On June 25, 1866, the office of chief justice was changed to that of county judge.

COUNTY JUDGES

John Rosenheimer
Elected June 25, 1866, and served from August 19, 1866 to August 28, 1868.

William K. Gamble
Appointed by General J. J. Reynolds on November 5, 1868, and served until his resignation on November 19, 1869.

H. Klocker
Appointed December 22, 1869 and served from January 3, 1870 to April 18, 1876.

Thomas A. Dwyer
Elected February 15, 1876 and served from April 18, 1876, to November 27, 1878.

Felix G. Smith
Elected November 5, 1878, and 1880 served from November 28, 1878 to December 31, 1882.

J. R. Mason
Elected November 7, 1882, and served from January 1, 1883, to December 31, 1884.

Charles L. Wurzbach
Elected November 4, 1884, 1886, and 1888 and served from January 1, 1885 to December 31, 1890.

Samuel W. McAllister
Elected November 4, 1889, and served from January 1, 1891 to December 31, 1892.

Bryan Callaghan
Elected November 8, 1892, 1894, and 1896 and served from January 1, 1893 to his resignation on February 18, 1897.

Peter Jonas
Appointed February 19, 1897, and served from February 19, 1897, to December 31, 1900.

Robert B. Green
Elected November 11, 1900, and 1902 and served from January 1, 1901 to December 31, 1906.

Phil H. Shook
Served from January 1, 1907, to December 31, 1912.

James R. Davis
Served from January 1, 1913, to December 31, 1920.

Augustus McClosky
Served from January 1, 1921, to December 31, 1928.

Perry S. Robertson
Served from January 1, 1929, to December 31, 1930.

William A. Wurzbach
Served from January 1, 1931, to December 31, 1932.

Frost Woodhull
Served from January 1, 1933, to December 31, 1936.

Egbert Schweppe
Served from January 1, 1937, to December 31, 1938.

Charles Anderson
Served from January 1, 1939, to August 14, 1964 (called to active duty during part of this time and A. M. Heck served until his return).

Jess W. Young
Appointed and served from August 18, 1964, to December 31, 1964.

Charles W. Grace
Elected and served from January 1, 1965 to December 31, 1966.

Blair Reeves
Served from January 1, 1967, to September 20, 1977, when he was appointed judge of County Court at Law No. 3.

A. J. Ploch
Appointed by Commissioners Court, when he resigned as County Commissioner for Precinct 4, and served from September 20, 1977, to his retirement in November 1978.

Albert Bustamante
Elected and served January 1, 1979, to January 18, 1984.

Leo Mendoza, Jr.
Appointed interim county judge and served from January 18, 1984, to November 14, 1984.

Tom Vickers
Elected and served from November 14, 1984, to January 16, 1991.

John A. Longoria
Appointed and served from January 16, 1991, to December 8, 1992.

Cyndi Taylor Krier
Elected and served from December 8, 1992 to May 8, 2001

Nelson W. Wolff
Appointed and elected, and served from May 8, 2001 to the present.

APPENDIX II

BEXAR COUNTY HISTORICAL COMMISSION MEMBERS
(AS OF OCTOBER 2004)

Felix Almaraz
Precinct 2

Judge James Barlow

Maria Alicia Burger
Precinct 4

Eleanor Foreman
Precinct 2

Theresa Gold
Precinct 2

Gary Houston
Precinct 4

Charles John
Precinct 3

Mickey Killian
Precinct 1

Federico Martinez
Precinct 1

Virginia Nicholas
Commission Chair
Appointed by county judge

Paul T. Ringenbach
Precinct 4

Francine L. Rowden
Precinct 3

Walt Schumann
Precinct 3

Lois Cooper White
Appointed by county judge

APPENDIX III

The Bexar County Coat-of-Arms with Crest

The shield is quartered into four parts. The first quarter, on the upper left, displays the arms of Don Alvaro de Zuniga, duke of Bejar, surmounted with the Gold Chain of Navarre. The Gold Chain of Navarre corresponds to our present-day United States Congressional Medal of Honor.

The second quarter, on the upper right, represents the work of the Spanish missionaries in New Spain. The Mission San Francisco de la Espada is a classic example of the architecture typical of Spanish mission churches. The blue field represents the church.

The third quarter, on the lower left, honors the Aztec Eagle of Mexico and the American Bald Eagle of the United States, both symbols of their respective countries. The green field represents the prosperity enjoyed by the people of Bexar.

The fourth quarter, on the lower right, commemorates the battles of the Republic of Texas for its independence, and the Lone Stat State's participation in the Civil War. The red field indicates that blood was shed. The silver star represents the Republic and the state and the cannon represents the battles. The cannon purposely faces the eagle in the third quarter, pointing out the fact that Texas fought wars with both Mexico and the United States. Over the shield, as a crest, is the crown of a duke of Spain, for which special permission was granted for its use since Bejar was named in honor of a duke.

On December 19, 1971, Don Fernando Muñoz Altea, king of arms to his Royal Highness, Prince Raniero Borbon Dos Sicilias of Spain, presented the coat-of-arms to the Honorable Blair Reeves, county judge of Bexar County. On December 22, 1971, the Bexar County Commissioners Court passed a resolution unanimously adopting the coat-of-arms as the official coat-of-arms for Bexar County. Through the efforts of the Texas Hispanic Foundation of San Antonio, with Adela M. Navarro, president; and Thomas A. Wilson, the coat-of-arms was designed and approved. The purpose of a coat-of-arms is to depict the history and heritage of its own in heraldic design.

The achievement as officially described are: Quarterly; first, argent, a bend sable, and orle, eight chain links, or, overall; second, azure, the Mission San Francisco de la Espada argent; third, vert, an eagle displayed, or; fourth, gules, a mullet, argent, and a wheeled cannon of the last. The crest: a ducal coronet, or.

Description courtesy of Alfred Rodriguez, Bexar County archivist.

About the Author

Joe Carroll Rust

Rust began his career in journalism at the age of fifteen, becoming a copyboy for the *San Antonio Light* while he was a freshman in high school. He rose through the ranks at the *Light*, as a general assignment reporter (before attending the University of Texas at Austin, where he received his degree in journalism), police reporter, courthouse reporter, political editor, editorial page editor, and associate editor. When the *Light* closed in 1993, Rust went to work for the *San Antonio Express-News* as a community relations specialist. He retired from the *Express-News* in 2001 and is now engaged in media consultation and part-time teaching.

About the Cover

Vanessa Lively

Vanessa Lively is an oil painter from San Antonio, Texas. She has studied under her mentor, Vie Dunn-Harr, and other artists at the Southwest School of Art and Craft, The University of Texas at San Antonio and San Antonio College.

Lively combines vivid color with organic form to express the abstract as well as other subjects including landscape, floral and portraiture. Her ability as an artist has been recognized throughout San Antonio and beyond. Vanessa is passionate about serving her community and people throughout the world. Recently, she has worked in this regard through fundraising events and other non-profit endeavors benefiting the underprivileged.

For more information about Lively and her work, please visit www.vanessalively.com.

Bexar County Courthouse *by Vanessa Lively. Oil on canvas, April 2004.*

For more information about the following publications or about publishing your own book, please call Historical Publishing Network at 800-749-9790 or visit www.lammertinc.com.

Black Gold: The Story of Texas Oil & Gas
Historic Abilene: An Illustrated History
Historic Amarillo: An Illustrated History
Historic Anchorage: An Illustrated History
Historic Austin: An Illustrated History
Historic Beaufort County: An Illustrated History
Historic Beaumont: An Illustrated History
Historic Bexar County: An Illustrated History
Historic Brazoria County: An Illustrated History
Historic Charlotte: An Illustrated History of Charlotte and Mecklenburg County
Historic Cheyenne: A History of the Magic City
Historic Comal County: An Illustrated History
Historic Corpus Christi: An Illustrated History
Historic Denton County: An Illustrated History
Historic Edmond: An Illustrated History
Historic El Paso: An Illustrated History
Historic Erie County: An Illustrated History
Historic Fairbanks: An Illustrated History
Historic Gainesville & Hall County: An Illustrated History
Historic Henry County: An Illustrated History
Historic Houston: An Illustrated History
Historic Illinois: An Illustrated History
Historic Kern County: An Illustrated History of Bakersfield and Kern County
Historic Laredo: An Illustrated History of Laredo & Webb County
Historic Louisiana: An Illustrated History
Historic Midland: An Illustrated History
Historic Montgomery County: An Illustrated History of Montgomery County, Texas
Historic Oklahoma: An Illustrated History
Historic Oklahoma County: An Illustrated History
Historic Omaha: An Illustrated History of Omaha and Douglas County
Historic Pasadena: An Illustrated History
Historic Passaic County: An Illustrated History
Historic Philadelphia: An Illustrated History
Historic Prescott: An Illustrated History of Prescott & Yavapai County
Historic Richardson: An Illustrated History
Historic Rio Grande Valley: An Illustrated History
Historic Scottsdale: A Life from the Land
Historic Shreveport-Bossier: An Illustrated History of Shreveport & Bossier City
Historic Texas: An Illustrated History
Historic Victoria: An Illustrated History
Historic Williamson County: An Illustrated History
Iron, Wood & Water: An Illustrated History of Lake Oswego
Miami's Historic Neighborhoods: A History of Community
Old Orange County Courthouse: A Centennial History
Plano: An Illustrated Chronicle
The New Frontier: A Contemporary History of Fort Worth & Tarrant County
The San Gabriel Valley: A 21st Century Portrait